FROM MY EYES, TO YOURS,

Through the Eyes of a
# BELFAST CHILD

TO PHYLLIS!

IN LIFE, WE ALL HAVE A CROSS TO
BEAR AND A VERY UNIQUE STORY TO
TELL; WE JUST HOPE THAT SOMEONE
WILL TAKE THE TIME TO LISTEN.
IT WAS CERTAINLY A PLEASURE TO
MEET YOU. THANK YOU SO MUCH, I
CERTAINLY HOPE THAT YOU ENJOY MY
"WEE" BOOK.
   CHEERS AND BEST WISHES!!

Printed in Canada by:

**Hignell Book Printing**
488 Burnell Street
Winnipeg, MB Canada R3G 2B4
www.hignell.mb.ca

Distributed to the trade by The Ingram Book Company

# Through the Eyes of a
# BELFAST CHILD

*Life. Personal Reflections. Poems.*

GREG MCVICKER

# Table of Contents

Acknowledgements . . . . . . . . . . . . . . . . . . . . . . . . . . . . . . . . . . . . . . . . i

Notes to the Reader. . . . . . . . . . . . . . . . . . . . . . . . . . . . . . . . . . . . . . vi

Scattered Youth . . . . . . . . . . . . . . . . . . . . . . . . . . . . . . . . . . . . . . . . . 1
    *Scattered Youth* . . . . . . . . . . . . . . . . . . . . . . . . . . . . . . . . . . . 31

Knockagh Monument . . . . . . . . . . . . . . . . . . . . . . . . . . . . . . . . . . .34
    *Knockagh Monument* . . . . . . . . . . . . . . . . . . . . . . . . . . . . . . 38

Stranger To My Land . . . . . . . . . . . . . . . . . . . . . . . . . . . . . . . . . . . .41
    *Stranger to my Land.* . . . . . . . . . . . . . . . . . . . . . . . . . . . . . . . 45

Hallows' Eve . . . . . . . . . . . . . . . . . . . . . . . . . . . . . . . . . . . . . . . . . .47
    *Hallows' Eve* . . . . . . . . . . . . . . . . . . . . . . . . . . . . . . . . . . . . . 52

The Socialization of Hate . . . . . . . . . . . . . . . . . . . . . . . . . . . . . . . .54

The Confessional . . . . . . . . . . . . . . . . . . . . . . . . . . . . . . . . . . . . . . .57
    *The Confessional.* . . . . . . . . . . . . . . . . . . . . . . . . . . . . . . . . . 63

An Ode to My Aunt Sadie . . . . . . . . . . . . . . . . . . . . . . . . . . . . . . . .65
    *An Ode to my Aunt Sadie.* . . . . . . . . . . . . . . . . . . . . . . . . . . . 67

Whispers in the Breeze. . . . . . . . . . . . . . . . . . . . . . . . . . . . . . . . . . .70
    *Whispers in the Breeze* . . . . . . . . . . . . . . . . . . . . . . . . . . . . . 73

The Enchantment of Achill. . . . . . . . . . . . . . . . . . . . . . . . . . . . . . . .75
    *The Enchantment of Achill* . . . . . . . . . . . . . . . . . . . . . . . . . . 78

In The Name of Religion. . . . . . . . . . . . . . . . . . . . . . . . . . . . . . . . . .81

Shenanigans of the Scattered Youth . . . . . . . . . . . . . . . . . . . . . . . .85
    *Belfast Telegraph* . . . . . . . . . . . . . . . . . . . . . . . . . . . . . . . . . 85
    *Kamikaze Catwalks.* . . . . . . . . . . . . . . . . . . . . . . . . . . . . . . . 87
    *Man in the Coveralls* . . . . . . . . . . . . . . . . . . . . . . . . . . . . . . 89
    *Escape from Carrick Castle* . . . . . . . . . . . . . . . . . . . . . . . . . 92
    *Car on the Beak* . . . . . . . . . . . . . . . . . . . . . . . . . . . . . . . . . 95

Belfast Craic . . . . . . . . . . . . . . . . . . . . . . . . . . . . . . . . . . . . . . . . . .98
    *Belfast Craic.* . . . . . . . . . . . . . . . . . . . . . . . . . . . . . . . . . . . 106

The Pulse of Derrylin . . . . . . . . . . . . . . . . . . . . . . . . . . . . . . . . . . .108
    *The Pulse of Derrylin.* . . . . . . . . . . . . . . . . . . . . . . . . . . . . . 120

Mum's Lament. . . . . . . . . . . . . . . . . . . . . . . . . . . . . . . . . . . . . . . .127
    *Mum's Lament* . . . . . . . . . . . . . . . . . . . . . . . . . . . . . . . . . . 135

From a Child to the Man . . . . . . . . . . . . . . . . . . . . . . . . . . . . . . . .138

Imagine That . . . . . . . . . . . . . . . . . . . . . . . . . . . . . . . . . . . . . . . . .146
    *Imagine That...* . . . . . . . . . . . . . . . . . . . . . . . . . . . . . . . . . . 149

C'est La Vie . . . . . . . . . . . . . . . . . . . . . . . . . . . . . . . . . . . . . . . .151
   *C'est La Vie* . . . . . . . . . . . . . . . . . . . . . . . . . . . . . . . . . .*153*

Taking a Stand . . . . . . . . . . . . . . . . . . . . . . . . . . . . . . . . . . . . . . .155

Alcohol Saviour . . . . . . . . . . . . . . . . . . . . . . . . . . . . . . . . . . . . . .159
   *Alcohol Saviour.* . . . . . . . . . . . . . . . . . . . . . . . . . . . . . . . . .*161*

A New Beginning . . . . . . . . . . . . . . . . . . . . . . . . . . . . . . . . . . . . .163
   *A New Beginning* . . . . . . . . . . . . . . . . . . . . . . . . . . . . . . . . .*167*

And We Call Ourselves Human? . . . . . . . . . . . . . . . . . . . . . . . . .169

Cry of the Wild . . . . . . . . . . . . . . . . . . . . . . . . . . . . . . . . . . . . . . .172
   *Cry of the Wild.* . . . . . . . . . . . . . . . . . . . . . . . . . . . . . . . . .*175*

Whose "Home and Native Land?". . . . . . . . . . . . . . . . . . . . . . . .177

Hearts Entwined . . . . . . . . . . . . . . . . . . . . . . . . . . . . . . . . . . . . .181
   *Hearts Entwined* . . . . . . . . . . . . . . . . . . . . . . . . . . . . . . . . .*183*

Little Angel . . . . . . . . . . . . . . . . . . . . . . . . . . . . . . . . . . . . . . . . .185
   *Little Angel* . . . . . . . . . . . . . . . . . . . . . . . . . . . . . . . . . . . .*188*

Lament for a Child. . . . . . . . . . . . . . . . . . . . . . . . . . . . . . . . . . . .191
   *Lament for a Child* . . . . . . . . . . . . . . . . . . . . . . . . . . . . . . . .*193*

Empty Promises . . . . . . . . . . . . . . . . . . . . . . . . . . . . . . . . . . . . .196
   *Empty Promises* . . . . . . . . . . . . . . . . . . . . . . . . . . . . . . . . . .*198*

Bruised and Battered . . . . . . . . . . . . . . . . . . . . . . . . . . . . . . . . . .200
   *Bruised and Battered* . . . . . . . . . . . . . . . . . . . . . . . . . . . . . .*204*

Hate Crimes Against Humanity . . . . . . . . . . . . . . . . . . . . . . . . .207

Disposable Humans . . . . . . . . . . . . . . . . . . . . . . . . . . . . . . . . . .209
   *Disposable Human* . . . . . . . . . . . . . . . . . . . . . . . . . . . . . . . .*212*

Surreal, Nine One One . . . . . . . . . . . . . . . . . . . . . . . . . . . . . . . .214
   *Surreal, Nine One One* . . . . . . . . . . . . . . . . . . . . . . . . . . . . .*217*

Going Forward in Reverse . . . . . . . . . . . . . . . . . . . . . . . . . . . . . .218
   *Going Forward in Reverse* . . . . . . . . . . . . . . . . . . . . . . . . . . .*220*

A Time to Reflect . . . . . . . . . . . . . . . . . . . . . . . . . . . . . . . . . . . .222

Brandy . . . . . . . . . . . . . . . . . . . . . . . . . . . . . . . . . . . . . . . . . . . .229

With Love from an Irish Mother. . . . . . . . . . . . . . . . . . . . . . . . . .241

One Final Thought . . . . . . . . . . . . . . . . . . . . . . . . . . . . . . . . . . .258

Godspeed, Madiba . . . . . . . . . . . . . . . . . . . . . . . . . . . . . . . . . . .274

Special Note to the Reader . . . . . . . . . . . . . . . . . . . . . . . . . . . . .278

About the Author. . . . . . . . . . . . . . . . . . . . . . . . . . . . . . . . . . . . .279

Connect with the Author . . . . . . . . . . . . . . . . . . . . . . . . . . . . . . .281

# Acknowledgements

THERE ARE COUNTLESS people who need to be thanked for their support in the development of this book, including those who have had the profound strength and unwavering courage to share their personal stories with me. It is from *their* experiences I've learned that countless others go through similar or differing traumas, which highlight the discrepancies that exist in the human journey of life. Whether reflecting on past negative experiences or present-day realities, I was driven to write about numerous issues around the world as seen through my own eyes. Not every experience is traumatic, however, and as such, I've tried to capture a delicate balance between these pages.

In my professional career as a social worker, I've learned that there is always a glimmer of hope that someone will take the time to listen to a person's painful story and offer solace, comfort, and support, or perhaps help the individual find light at the end of an arduous and difficult journey. Sadly, there are those who may never see that day, as they feel so controlled, trapped, or helpless within their environment that they are terrified to seek assistance for fear of retribution.

For years prior to penning this book, I wrote poems about various experiences. While speaking to my dear friend Melanie who was undergoing her own personal difficulties, she asked if I would let her read a sample of my poetic compositions. One that touched her most was "Mum's Lament," which she said I had written about her beloved father. Although she did not need my permission whatsoever, she believed this gave her the ability to recognize her strengths, and it provided her with an opportunity to begin a journey of healing through introspection. Melanie encouraged me to write more, as she felt others could see themselves in my thoughts.

Another wonderful friend who I've had the pleasure of knowing for over twenty years called Patricia, had an extremely traumatic upbringing as presented under the guise of a traditional, patriarchial family unit. As she read "Bruised and Battered," she visualized the events occurring and was infuriated by the actions of the male while wanting to help the female whom the reflection and poem are based upon. In her words, "I wanted to climb through the page and knock some sense into him while helping her get out from under his authority." By her own admission, Patricia's family wanted her to follow their cultural ideologies, whereby women are treated as second-class citizens and are expected to follow patriarchal directives. She challenged these norms and has since moved to be out from under those bitter influences and live life how *she* chooses, not by some outdated belief or authority system.

As humans we all have a story to tell, but when hearing someone else's difficult journey, we can find strength, encouragement, and inspiration within their words and apply those teachings to our own daily struggles. There are those who are much better or worse off than we are, but we all have a cross to bear. As I have learned through my own path in life and from countless experiences whether positive or negative, laughter and humour are some of the best medicines we have at our disposal. This provides us with an opportunity to at least smile, even if only temporarily.

My hope is that those of you who read this book take time to reflect upon yourself or others within your social circles who have had the courage to share their journey; to look deeper into what was used as a coping mechanism in addressing those issues and what can be done to make change for the greater good. You may also find comfort in knowing you are not alone. Simply writing about such issues does not provide me with any immunity from them or their impact.

My biggest inspiration for writing this book is my mum. She encouraged me to embrace this writing gift and would spend countless hours going over my work, no matter how good or bad the piece started out. She helped me develop many of the pieces to the point as now presented within the following pages for you to read and reflect upon. Thank you, Mum, for all you have done for me over the years. Without your encouragement and guidance; without your support and love; and without your sacrifices while growing up in bitter, war torn Northern Ireland; none of this would ever have been possible. You gave us everything and asked for nothing in return but our love.

My daughter, Caitlin, who is currently in her third year at the university of Winnipeg and still exploring her options.

I have to thank my dad, Charles McVicker, for his belief in his family. He spent years at sea and would send home his pay-packet to keep us alive. Growing up during "The Troubles"

My son, Ciarán. As a goalie of six years, his most respected player in the NHL is Jonathan Quick of the Los Angeles Kings. Ciarán hopes to follow in his skates one day and play at this elite level of hockey!

remains a large part of who we are. Our bloodied history, both political and religious, kept him from finding work in our native homeland. Although we were not involved in the conflict and had absolutely no interest in it, we were always directly impacted by the ignorance of others. As a result, we only saw my father two weeks out of every year. Thank you, Dad, for all you have done.

I'd like to give a special mention to my sister, Karen McVicker, who on September 23, 2011, was diagnosed with Acute Lymphoblastic Leukemia. She spent an amazing amount of time and effort carefully articulating her courageous battle against this disease through social media, and remains a warrior, having successfully undergone a bone marrow transplant. She has met with her donor, to whom I would like to say thank you from the bottom of my heart for giving my sister a second chance at life. I would also like to give a mention to her co-workers, who embrace the true spirit of humanity and go to great lengths to help her out while she continues her battle. You all know who you are and in my eyes, are truly special!

My wish remains that one day, Karen will take the time to write a full memoir of her journey, as she could inspire an entire generation of people who unfortunately may also have to face a chronic illness. Karen is a published author, a fantastic artist, and a survivor! But to understand where she found her strength, one really only has to look at our mum and the gifts she gave us to overcome any challenge.

Caitlin and Ciarán, my two beautiful children, have been a tremendous support to me while writing this book. As a parent, I have learned so much from them both over the years and have seen through the innocence of their eyes. Thank you for being such amazing and wonderful children. You leave me smiling to no end for all of your accomplishments in your young lives. You are my world, my life, and you mean absolutely everything to me. You make me laugh, smile, and pick me up when the chips are down. I am truly blessed to call you my kids. Be sure to pursue your dreams. Cherish your Irish heritage.

I'd like to personally thank Molly Kavanagh, Melanie Chartrand, Teresa McAuley, Patricia Mancini Holt, Jean Camp, Ruth McDonald, Jade Harper, Angela Timchuk, Joe McVicker, Paul Devlin, Karl Milnes, Omar Hawash, William Falls, and Mark Rickerby for their unwavering words of encouragement, and for supporting me to write more.

To the entire Maher clan, Heath Finch, Rosie Henderson, Tara Cahill, Kathleen Lebel, and Jeff Sweetland, thank you all for being a special part of our family. And for those colleagues who I wanted to acknowledge but asked that I not publish their names, I thank each of you for your guidance and insights. You also know who you are.

Finally, I would like to offer my heartfelt and sincerest appreciation to my dear friend, Marianne Curran, for taking the time to review my manuscript and give it a fresh look through the eyes of an Irish lady. Thank you for spending countless hours on the phone to provide me with your motivating insights. Your feedback has been invaluable, for which I am forever grateful.

Cheers!
Greg.

# Notes to the Reader

I HAD OFTEN THOUGHT about writing a book, but never took the challenge seriously until one day in August of 2010. Unbeknownst to me at the time, this would take more than three years to complete, but realistically has been fifteen years in the making.

Although the poems are based on my own experiences—being born and raised in Belfast, Northern Ireland, and having to leave my country due to the political and religious persecutions my family faced; then to my experiences in Canada, where I have lived for the past twenty-eight years—I have also written about people who came into my life or shared their stories with me. These include things I have seen through my own eyes, such as the difficulties and challenges people face throughout this world regardless of their gender, race, stature, cultural background, geographical location, or social standing.

I struggled to find a sense of identity growing up, as I was labeled through the lens of others based on their ignorance and hatred as passed down through generations. Through this book I have begun looking at my lifelong quest to try to find out who I am and where I belong, as I do not identity with religious views, political rubbish, or other social constructs that try to place me in pre-determined categories.

One thing I'd like to note is that I have written this not so much as a narrative as is seen in other books. What I have tried to do is write this using the Irish method of storytelling, as if I was sitting directly across from you and speaking. There are those who refer to this as having the "Gift of the Gab."

I have seen and heard though the First Nations population, whom I have the honour and blessing of working with daily, several parallels in comparison between the struggles their people went through at the hands of their colonizers, to that of what the Irish faced. People from differing nations and all walks of life come together in sharing circles and listen to one person tell a story while holding an eagle's feather or talking stick. I've very much done the same here in that each composition takes you through different areas of my life at various intervals, and how the knowledge gained from these experiences applies to the defining of my worldview.

I've included six compositions I wrote in the final year of my social work degree, as I see their relevancy when compared to the nature of the issues regarding global inequities that I've tried to address. Unfortunately, six years on, not much has changed.

Although dedications are included within each reflection to those who are or have been a part of my life, this book is dedicated in its entirety to the beloved memory of my Mum, Catherine Philomena McVicker (nee Devlin), and all she stood for. As captured within her In Memoriam notices, published each year and in the language of our ancestors:

*Mna na hÉireann, mo mháthair, mo chroí, tá tú go hálainn.*
*(Woman of Ireland, my mother, my love, you are beautiful).*

Finally, to those of you who have had negative experiences in life and seek change from past sufferings, to those of you who understand what homesickness is all about (as I suffered immensely from it for eighteen years), to those who are trying to understand your spiritual side, and to those who do not believe you can make a difference in the life of another, I offer you these words:

*Cuir do lámh i mo láimh, agus ná féach siar go deo.*
*(Put your hand in my hand, and never look back).*

I would love to hear your story, for who knows what kind of higher learning or healing can come from it, or perhaps how it can help influence someone else in knowing they are not alone in their journey. We can all learn from each other and apply similar experiences to the greater good for all humankind. My contact information is at the back of this book. In the meantime, I hope you enjoy reading this as much as I enjoyed writing it.

*Sláinte, mo chara! / Health, my friend!*
*Greg McVicker, BSW.*

M Y STORY BEGINS on a sunny day in 1985, when I faced one of the toughest moments in my short fifteen-year existence. I had to say goodbye not only to my best friend called Denis, but also to everything that was near and dear to my heart. My mum and dad had told me I was to forget all I knew, as my life was going to start all over again. We were uprooting and moving.

Denis became my best friend at an early age. He and his family had become a part of my life when we attended primary school together in Northern Ireland. We lived in the Knockview area, from which he and his family lived within a ten-minute walk. Our homes were made of brick and mortar, and had slate roofs, along with gardens and rosebushes that were carefully groomed. Coal or oil was used for heating, along with an electric fireplace to take the chill out of the Irish air.

He and I would walk home in the afternoons with his mum and siblings, as Denis's house was just outside of what was once our peaceful, middle-class neighbourhood of Newtownabbey. This district was made up of families from both sides of the religious community, but without the sectarian violence we witnessed daily on the evening news.

After dropping me off, I would stand on our back doorstep, and, along with my mum, I would wave to them as they walked along the Doagh Road before disappearing out of sight. A few years later they would move to the Woodford area, which was around the corner from our school. Later, this would become my introduction to many of our friends who also resided in this area.

For one year, my siblings and I knew the day of our immigration was fast approaching. The date was July 19, a day normally associated with my dad's birthday, but now also with the day of our relocation to Canada. The struggles leading up to this were immensely difficult to deal with, as my parents asked us to keep our pending move to ourselves. I was haunted by this and struggled to compose myself when telling Denis about it in private before eventually sharing it with the rest of my mates while standing on the corner of Woodford Drive and Woodford Park. Denis and I had discussed this before I made the official announcement. The problem was that we often spoke in secrecy about it. We didn't think it to be fair to our other friends, who were very much a part of our social circles but were being excluded from our conversations on the basis that we were not to say anything to anyone. Shock and awe rippled throughout our chatter that evening after I broke my silence.

The decision for this move was made in 1984 after my mum and dad had chanced upon a three-week holiday with two of my aunts and uncles who were already settled in Winnipeg, Canada, and had been for many years. My parents found the freedoms something to be very thankful for as we had faced years of trauma and persecution in the only land we knew: Northern Ireland.

We were not part of any sectarian movements. We were not involved in the bombings that became a daily part of our very beings after we started attending secondary and grammar schools outside the safety of our neighbourhood. We had no political affiliation nor were such views ever allowed to cross the doorstep of our middle-class home. No matter our attempts to keep ourselves free from the bitterness and cancerous hatred in Belfast that we were somewhat removed from, we were always affected and impacted by it. This became amplified after council houses were built just beyond the perimeter of our enclave. Our status as untouchable from the persecution of taunting, name-calling, or being stopped on the streets had come to an end. After being questioned about our backgrounds by individuals from the other side of the religious community regarding what church we attended, where we lived, or what school we went to, we'd end up getting punched, kicked, or pushed off of our bicycles as a result of our honest answers.

On the night of July 16, 1985 I was out with Richard, who was another good friend of mine from Woodford. At around 9pm, he walked me down and left me off at the **SADOW** at the bottom of Woodford Road, which was also known by its full name: the **S**mokers **A**nd **D**rinkers **O**nly **W**all. Although this was named by my brother Joe and his mates, it stuck with us all. It was where Joe, his mates and eventually my friends and I could do as the name suggests – smoke and drink out of sight.

The SADOW was a field located along the Doagh Road, joining the Knockview and Woodford area together. This is where we spent many nights and weekends growing into our teenage years, getting into countless fights with those from the council housing district, who had nothing but loathing in their view for those from outside of their own pungent enclave. Although not everyone from this area can be painted with the same brush, those that came into our inner circles carried this same bitterness with them no matter where they went or who they met.

I crossed the SADOW but stopped halfway over and decided that I also needed to say goodbye to other friends of mine, who were leaving the following morning for holidays in France. I would be long gone before they returned and wanted them to remember me. This was our last chance to say goodbye to each other, as I never knew when I'd ever see any of them again.

I met the youngest lad Andrew at the end of his family's driveway. He led me to the back of their house to where everyone was already gathered. I said hello to each of them. Elaine, June, and Judith were standing on the back porch with Nicola, who would often come down from the Glebe district approximately two-and-a-half miles from our home. Was it coincidence they all stood there awaiting my arrival? I never asked, and to this day still do not know, but I spoke with them all, including their parents.

It was a tearful night, as I knew my time in my homeland was drawing to a close and that within three days I wouldn't see them out on our streets any longer. I did not want to go and wished I could have jumped on the ferry with them to escape my pending move.

After saying my final goodbye, Andrew accompanied me out to the end of the driveway. I walked along Woodford Park and made my way towards the SADOW. Unbeknownst to me at the time, Andrew had quietly followed me. He watched as I put my hands to my head while I gazed off towards the night sky. I was lost deep in thought, struggling with the idea that I did not know when I would see my friends again. Andrew did not believe me when I told his siblings that I was moving. He thought that I was trying to pull the same wool over his eyes as other friends had done when they were leaving for family holidays to Spain, but would tell him that they were moving away and would not be coming back.

After they left the following morning, I wrote my name in giant letters on the tarmac directly across from where Denis lived in the Woodford area. This would be later eulogized in a tongue-in-cheek letter from Nicola that read, "It's really hard to forget you as there is a massive **GREG** scrawled

This is my granny, my uncle Jimmy, my mum, and my aunt Josephine all together in 1985, one-week prior to us leaving for Canada. Almost twenty-six years after our departure, they have all been reunited and watch over me every day.

on the footpath." I felt I'd left my mark, at least until the next torrential downpour erased my memory from their minds. I still have all the letters I received from them tucked away in a shoebox, as I hoped one day we would all get together to look back on our letters while laughing at our childhood innocence and cheek.

Even before we left for Canada, my troubles began. On the night of July 18, and after Denis and Richard had walked me home from Woodford, I went into our bare house. The only thing left for me to stare at or appreciate was the carpet on the floor that would double as my bed, since everything else had been shipped overseas. Yet not even a week before, on the eve of July 13, we were all laughing and mucking around while sharing in a celebration, as my parents had an open house for family who came by for a farewell bash.

There was plenty of alcohol to be had. Denis and I happily helped ourselves to this. I snuck several tins out to the front street and out of my parent's view for us to drink. Harp lager became a favourite for us, along with whatever I could get my hands on and subsequently dump into our guts. After downing each drink, I'd go back into our house and tell the adults that Joe and his mates, who were near legal age, wanted a few drinks, and that I was their messenger. I did not inform them that the plan was for me to go back outside and celebrate with Denis with a cache of free booze. I had a denim jacket with inside pockets, so I'd place an extra few tins inside to avoid having to make so many trips and hopefully not have anyone become suspicious of my frequent visits.

Since I grabbed whatever was available and made a hurried exit each time, we ended up selling two of the four tins of Guinness I'd pinched to two wee lads we knew from the area for 50p each. We could not stand our first taste of this famous stout, and wanted to recoup our losses. We'd nothing to lose and everything to gain—including getting polluted for free.

This night was different though. After getting home and putting my head down on the bare carpet within the empty shell of what we once knew as our house, I called my mum and dad every name imaginable while I slept. The following morning they would be taking me away from my homeland, my friends, and my childhood. I've no recollection of doing so, but my parents never forgot it. They often questioned themselves as to whether or not they had made the right decision, since I had become so bitter and angry toward them.

July 19 marked a few occasions for me. The day I would get onto an airplane for the very first time. The day my life would forever be changed, trying to find a lost identity that I never really knew, aside from how I had defined it among my mates. I became caught between two worlds and did not know which one I belonged in. I wanted to stay in my country, no matter how much the surrounding environment—its hatred, political wars, and religious views—impacted me while growing up. This was where my heart belonged. And so that morning I begged my mum to leave me to live with my Uncle Jimmy in Belfast, who I argued could take care of me while I finished school.

My uncle Barney and my cousin Mark, who came over from England to buy my parents' car, came around to pick us up. They loaded our suitcases and remaining items into one of the two cars. Since my pleas fell on deaf ears, Denis, Richard, and I went to tour the grounds of our neighbourhood one last time. I vowed it would not be long before they saw my face again. At the time, however, I did not realize this would not occur until seven years later, and at that time would be very much incomplete. Richard had by then joined the army and gone to serve his mission overseas. I often pondered his decision to do so, but it was not my place to question his direction in life.

After being loaded into the cars and beginning the trek outwards from our house, I looked back at my mates, catching the outlines of their wristbands, jeans, t-shirts, and their headbanger mops of hair. This image was to be an everlasting one in my mind.

We took what seemed to be the ride of doom to Belfast International Airport for one final and tearful farewell to all of our family that had come to see us off. From there and after going through the security checkpoint and after being cleared for boarding, we walked down the ramp to the plane, got buckled in, and waved goodbye to our beloved land. I watched as people fussed about loading luggage into overhead bins or pulled magazines to pass the time.

Although I had turned fifteen only four days before, I'd no idea what to expect and wondered why vomit bags were inside the seat pocket in front of me. My mum laughed at me as we taxied away from the gate and the pilots put the engines into full throttle, preparing for take-off. I panicked and began yelping while watching the concrete disappear from beneath us.

Rolling green fields along with mountainous terrain and Irish loughs disappeared when we rose above the fluffy cloud cover, which so often held rains that soaked the lush landscape below. All I could see out the window was a blue sky. My home and native land were completely gone from sight, but not from my heart. I was already planning my return trip home, even though we had only been in the air for about a half-hour by this point.

People were allowed to smoke on the plane, and the thick, stale air it created would choke the life out of anyone caught in its path. It caused such a blue haze that it was difficult to watch the movie. My eyes watered. I decided to get up and go to the bathroom halfway towards the back of the plane. It was very busy, and an American man said to me in his thick, southern accent, "You'd need a nickel to use the washroom around here."

Since this was my first time flying and as I did not know what the man meant by his statement, I bolted back to my seat. "Ma, some American back there says I need a nickel to use the bogs. What does he mean by a nickel? Where do I get one of those?"

My mum found this to be quite humourous, although I was personally not impressed since I needed to go to the bog really badly and didn't want to be on the plane in the first place.

After about eight hours flying across the length of Ireland and over the Atlantic Ocean and eastern seaboard, we landed in the "capital" of Canada: Toronto. As this was five hours behind us, I was knackered. We had to stand around while my mum and dad went through the process of clearing customs and our landing papers before we could catch our next flight.

While they were doing that, I decided to wander around the airport. I stopped at a water fountain to get a drink but found it to be completely disgusting. It was not from home and carried a very different taste that my palate was not used to. Life here was already making a negative impression, but I really wasn't giving the first few hours a chance, and we hadn't stepped foot outside an airport at this stage. We were in transit to our destination and what would become our new home.

Finally, at 6pm on July 19, 1985 and on the very same day we'd left behind our beloved country, we landed in Winnipeg and were immediately greeted by our large family, including my aunt, two uncles and numerous cousins I'd never met before. With the exception of my mum's sister, Maureen, and my uncle Malcolm, both of whom I'd last seen in 1981 when along with my cousin, Treasaigh,

**The very first photograph taken shortly after our arrival in Canada. We were met by my aunt, my uncles, and my cousins, along with a very hot day, which was something that we were not used to. Pictured left to right are: my aunt Maureen, Larry, my cousins Maria and Jim, my mum, my uncle Malcolm, my cousin Patrick, my brother Joe, my uncle John, me (doing my best Angus Young impersonation), and my sister, Karen.**

had moved back to Northern Ireland, everyone else had Canadian accents that sounded both funny and weird to me. They spoke at about the same pace as a snail crawls compared to our way of speaking, which is approximately two notches down from the speed of sound.

Aside from jeans, their style of clothing was different from anything I had ever seen before, which left me wondering how on earth I was to adapt to this county. There was no way I would dress the same way as everyone else. I wanted to go back to the airport I had just come out of and catch the first plane home to tell my friends that my pending move was a complete hoax.

When we stepped outside, it was a bright, sunny, hot day. My first thought after collecting our bags and walking towards the carpark to our transportation was, "Warm wind? How the hell do you get warm wind?" We had never experienced this before. It was always bloody freezing in Ireland!

At first glance, the landscape had no appeal or attraction to it whatsoever. There weren't any mountains or lush green grass. No sheep causing traffic jams, double-decker buses driving around, or rolling hills to climb. The scenery was flat, drab, and very bland compared to Ireland. Winnipeg lies in the middle of the prairies within the province of Manitoba. Basically the best way to describe it is that if your dog were to run away, you could watch it do so for three days.

There were no streams, no castles, no loughs, and no ferries. The place was a concrete jungle filled with skyscrapers, train tracks, and people who drove on the wrong side of the road. Vehicles had something called an 8-track, which took cartridges bigger than our Atari. Cars were parked in one direction along the same side of the street, which actually seemed preferable, since people could walk up the footpath without having to step foot onto the road to get around them. Yet this was so far removed from home that somehow I knew trying to blend in to this country was going to be a cultural shock.

After driving around in a blistering hot vehicle with the windows rolled down to act as air conditioning and going to a drive-thru beer vendor to pick up a few cases of Club for my cousins, we arrived at my Aunt Maureen's house. She promptly asked if I'd like something to drink before saying, "Do you want some root beer?"

I responded, "Aye, I'll take some root beer!" and thought about how brilliant my aunt was for getting us such a product. Beer! I neglected to ask what she meant by the word "root," although I was not worried about it since I had freely drank to my heart's content the week before and no one had said anything about it. Then again, they did not know about my antics on our front street. Nor was she offering me Guinness, so I thought I was in good standing.

Needless to say, after she poured the glass of fizzy, foamy drink, I choked on it before spitting it out. I asked if that was how beer tasted in this country – like Tiger Balm. It was nothing like I had ever tasted before, and I would certainly avoid at all costs. Putrid wouldn't have come close to describing it.

Adjusting to life proved to be a tremendous struggle. Trying to fit into a land that I had no understanding of or appreciation for proved difficult. The furthest I'd been from my district was in 1981 when we went over to Iverness, Scotland to visit my dad, who was in from sea after returning from the Falklands War. This was a brutal time in our lives. There were more than enough close calls for my dad, as their supply ship had artillery shells rain down upon it. From there we traveled down to see my aunt, who lived in England.

It was going to be a social struggle for me to try to learn the ways of life (as taken for granted by those who lived within the shores of this country), since it was so far removed from everything I had ever known.

When my parents came over in 1984 to look at the possibility of moving to Canada, they were also considering New Zealand and England. My mum felt New Zealand was too far from home and that we might experience difficulty from having Belfast accents and due to "The Troubles" if we were to move to England.

After their holiday, my parents decided the City of Winnipeg, which has been the World's Slurpee capital for fourteen years running, would become our home.

Speaking of Slurpees, I had only been in the city for two days at this time, but as I had brought some pounds over with me, I decided to exchange them into local currency at the Bank of Montreal located on the corner of Osborne Street and Morley Avenue. The paper money was smaller than the pounds we used, and trying to understand what was a quarter, a dime, or that bloody nickel (as the American man told me I needed to use the bog on the flight over) proved to be yet another challenge.

From there, I made my way over to the 7-11 and wanted to get a Slurpee. My mum had shown us pictures of them and had told us about how great they were and tasted. As much as I dreaded our move, I was definitely anticipating my first taste of this icy treat.

I walked into the 7-11 and approached the cash register and asked the sales clerk, "Do you sell Slurpees?" He pointed behind me and said they were on the other side of the counter. "Great," I thought, walking around to get one while licking my chops. However, I came across several machines with spinning wheels, white and blue levers, and a coloured ice-looking type liquid swooshing around behind windows that had different flavours listed on top of them. These contraptions were completely foreign to me, and for all I knew, could have been part of a scientific experiment conducted by NASA.

I stared in awe for a moment before looking back and forth between the machines and their contents. From there I made my way back over to the counter to the same sales clerk whom I'd spoken to five minutes before and asked, "Can you please show me how to make a Slurpee?"

The clerk must have thought I was either having him on, or perhaps from the sound of my accent realized I was definitely not from this part of the world. It was not as if he was up to his eyeballs serving customers as I was the only person in the store.

He shuffled his way over to the machines, and in a slow, deliberate, and almost taunting voice began showing me the steps as if he were talking to a young child.

> "You decide what size of Slurpee you want. Look up above you and you can see the prices. You then take whatever size of cup you want and put it under the spout. Do you see this lever? Move it from the left to the right and that will allow the Slurpee to go into the cup. When you close the lever the Slurpee will stop flowing. You can add another flavour if you like. After the cup is full, take a lid, put it on top, and get yourself a straw. Then come over to the counter and pay for it. That is how you make a Slurpee. Understood?"

I nodded, but did not pay much attention to him making fun of me. At the time, I did not realize he was doing this, since I was so busy salivating as if I were a dog waiting for a meaty bone from its owner. This was something I could write about in my letters to my mates to tell them all about my new-found experiences.

I don't think my mates were as excited as I was, as I wrote about the various flavours I'd buy at every opportunity and would try out several combinations (with the exception of body-rub-flavoured root beer), only to end up with a sugar high and something else I'd never experienced before: brain freeze. Those hurt, and I'm sure I must have looked like a right eejit on more occasions than not, especially when walking around with my face screwed up and my hand squeezing my forehead when drinking Slurpees in the middle of winter. I tried a beer-flavoured Slurpee once, but that was made by my own hand after attending a party.

About a week after arriving, my cousin Patrick had stopped over at my Aunt Maureen's house and asked if I wanted to go with him to a place called Thunderbird Billiards for a few games of pool. We used go to the 147 in Belfast to play (this is the name given to the highest score a player can attain in a game of snooker), so I thought this would be great. We were fans of several of the world's greatest players back home and often marveled at their skills as we watched them on TV. It would also give me the chance to get to know one of my cousins, whom I hadn't met prior to landing— they'd immigrated to Canada in 1970 at the beginning of "The Troubles."

After walking along Walker Avenue and reaching Osborne Street, we turned the corner to make our way over to the pool hall. Upon looking up at a sign posted outside a building on the same side of the street as we were on, I froze in my tracks. Without thinking, I looked at the busy street beside me and, not taking into account the amount of traffic flow (all of which was coming and going in a direction completely opposite to that which I was accustomed to), I ran across the street, all the while dodging vehicles until I got to the other side.

I heard my cousin screaming after me, his voice peppered with colourful swear words asking where I was going and what I was doing. As I was running, I shouted that I'd meet him at the pool hall. Once on the opposite footpath, I made my way up the road and waited for him outside the Park Theatre. Patrick walked up the street opposite to where I was standing, crossed Rathgar Avenue, and joined up with me again.

"Greg, what the fuck are you thinking? You're in Canada now. This isn't Ireland. You can't go jaywalking over here like you do back home. Do you see this thing here?" He pointed to a large button attached to a lamppost of sorts. "This is a pedestrian crosswalk. Here in Winnipeg, you press this button to activate the lights. You wait for the traffic to stop. THEN you cross the street."

Still breathless from playing a real life version of Frogger, I exclaimed, "Aye right. We've those things too. They're called zebra crossings. But I can't be over on that side of the street!"

Patrick looked at me with his eyebrows furrowed and said "WHAT?"

I repeated, "I can't be over on that side of the street because of that store right there." I pointed to the sign that had made me freeze before bolting. "I was warned about those places just last week and was told Canada has lots of them so to avoid them at all costs."

Patrick, obviously still quite dumbfounded, looked back to the strip of shops that lined the streets, including a Warehouse One, a Royal Bank, and a store that sold carpets. "What store are you talking about?"

"Do you see that store right there with red lettering on the sign? That's a bad place. They sell drugs. I was warned about those places and was told to stay away from them."

Patrick looked at me, completely exasperated, and said, "What? Are you talking about Metro Drugs? For Jesus sakes, Greg. Do you not know what that is? It's a pharmacy, you flippin' eejit!"

I looked back at him and said, "WHAT DO YOU MEAN? WHY WOULDN'T THEY CALL IT THAT THEN? They're called chemists. If it had of said chemists, or a friggin' pharmacy for that matter, I wouldn't have near half killed myself running across the bloody road to get away from the place."

What Patrick did not know was that on the night of July 16, when I went to visit my friends and said my final farewell before they left for France, their dad told me about how bad the drug problem was in Canada. I made a vow to him that I wouldn't use drugs and took his advice to avoid them at all costs. I was young, innocent, and a complete stranger in a strange land, taking words at face value without questioning their meaning. My other thought was that, as my mum used to tell me, I was as thick as pig's shite and here I was proving that very statement.

My early days in Winnipeg were not easy, as I got myself into a lot of trouble. One day in August of 1985, I snuck back into my Aunt Sadie and Uncle John's house after visiting them and before they were due to go out, and phoned my friends, as I knew Elaine and her family had returned from their holidays. Sure enough, they were all there, and we spent a good hour or two talking. I did not realize that phone companies documented all calls made from a landline. So when my aunt and uncle got their phone bill and seen the listing for a call to a number in Belfast, I was in deep shite with my parents. Live and learn? Not quite…

Adapting to school life here was just as painful as trying to find myself within this country. On my first day I was to attend Churchill High School, I was actually very excited. My mum had taken me down two weeks before to register, but I fought with her every step of the way against going into Grade Ten, since I would have only had one more year of secondary school had we have stayed in Belfast. I did not want to do three more years at school to get a Grade Twelve education, so opted for the two-year plan instead. This did not quite work out to my benefit. I miserably failed everything in my first year from a lack of interest, a lack of caring, and wanting to go back to my mates.

The reason for my excitement on my first morning of school was that I could put on a pair of jeans and a T-shirt and not have to worry about wearing a dress shirt, tie, blazer, slacks, polished shoes, or any other part of the uniform we had been forced to wear. I could also put on white socks (our secondary school had banned them, since they felt these challenged the appropriate attire that we were expected to wear). Boys found in breach of this policy would be grabbed by their ears, dragged into the school by our rotten bastard teachers, and strapped mercilessly. Our school systems were very much like the meat grinders depicted in the classic Pink Floyd song "Another Brick in the Wall."

After walking to school with my cousin Treasaigh, I presented myself at the office on the second floor to try and find out where I was to report. The information was given, and so I made my way downstairs to the lower level. Upon reaching the classroom, I was met at the front door by a man who went on to become one of my favourite teachers. However, during this first introduction and in his slow, growling, and methodical (almost robotic sounding) voice, he spoke to me through clenched teeth and said, "Are you supposed to be in this classroom?"

I responded that I had just been sent down from the office, and that this was where I was supposed to be. Obviously the teacher did not believe what I was saying, as his response was, "You sound like a foreigner to me. I don't think you are in the right class. You need to go back to the office and find out where you are supposed to be." Thinking back on that day, his voice reminds me of Professor Snape from the Harry Potter movies.

Given his direction, I turned on my heel and went up to the office to explain what the teacher had just told me. One of the staff members walked me back down to the same classroom, only this time I was allowed to enter. I suppose her explanation made much more sense to him than anything I had previously said.

I found a seat in the second to last vertical row and sat one seat back from the front of the classroom. From there I looked over to my right to see a girl I knew called Sherri was in the same class as me, so I nodded over to say hello. I became lost in my own thoughts at this point, as Sherri's brother Larry was married to my cousin Maria. He had always reminded me of the rock star Prince back in his *Purple Rain* days, although Larry didn't have a purple motorcycle or a horn-shaped guitar.

Suddenly I was snapped out of my daydreaming by a voice that had come literally out of nowhere and given a couple of announcements. I looked all around the classroom to try and determine the source of this, only to finally see a loudspeaker above the chalkboard.

Without any forewarning, every student suddenly jumped straight up and out of their seats, facing forwards, while my arse stayed firmly planted in my own seat. It was as if a call to military inspection was about to take place.

I looked around to see what the fuss was about as the crackle of a record came to life and started playing a song that I had never heard before! Still unaware of what was going on, I looked over at Sherri for a clue. She seemed aware that the teacher was shooting an evil eye in my immediate direction. Sherri mouthed the words "Stand up" while slowly making a gesture to the same effect with her left hand, making every attempt to not get caught.

I nodded and stood up, though I planted my arse on the end of the table attached to my chair, put my hands behind me, and half sprawled myself out. I still had no clue what was going on or what I was listening to. The teacher continued to watch me and was obviously very quickly losing his patience at my behaviour. He snapped his arms by his sides and expected me to stand to attention like a soldier. Although I did not realize it at the time, I was being disrespectful towards the Canadian national anthem, which was played every morning before classes began. Since we did not follow this practice in Belfast, I didn't see the necessity of it.

At the end of the anthem the person making the announcements asked everyone to remain standing for the Lord's Prayer. Knowing this along with the Hail Mary in my traditional tongue, I recited the Lord's Prayer in English and the Hail Mary in the language I was taught in secondary school and was expected to speak. I closed my eyes, crossed my thumbs over one another to make the sign of the cross, and began my recital:

*"Sé do bheatha, a Mhuire,*
*atá lán de ghrásta,*
*Tá an Tiarna leat.*
*Is beannaithe thú idir mná,*
*Agus is beannaithe toradh do bhroinne, Íosa.*
*A Naomh-Mhuire, a Mháthair Dé,*
*guigh orainn na peacaigh,*
*anois, agus ar uair ár mbáis. Amen."*

As I was coming to the tail end of the prayer, I opened my eyes and looked around at the entire classroom only to see that several students were either stunned, shocked, or in awe, all of whom were staring directly at me, their mouths hanging open. I had recited my Our Father in the time it took them to reach the end of the verse "And lead us not into temptation," and was already into my Hail Mary in my traditional language. I was simply doing what I knew and had been taught to do.

The classroom began to empty out, but upon looking at my schedule, I saw that my first class was math with none other than the same teacher who did not want me invading his space in the first place. As the room filled up, I stayed in the same chair I'd found that morning. Once everyone was seated and the lesson started, the teacher made no effort to look at anyone else but me. In his low growl, he asked, "Did they teach you about Pythagoras's theorem in that foreign place you came from?"

The answer was easy, as it had been severely beaten into us within our militant school system. Without blinking an eye, and brimming with excitement, I hurriedly responded,

"The square of the length of the hypotenuse of a right triangle equals the sum of the squares of the lengths of the other two sides."

A girl sitting to my immediate right and another girl who sat directly behind her blurted out in unison, "What did he just say?" while others sat just as stunned, with their eyes affixed upon me, jaws hanging. I thought to myself that not only was this going to be a long day, it was going to be a long life of trying to fit in. It was already starting to lose its appeal—the appeal of not having to wear a school uniform ever again. At that moment I wished I could leave and head overseas where I wouldn't face these troubles, even if it meant I had to wear an ugly blazer with a school crest on the pocket, trousers, dress shoes, and a hideous tie at my shite school.

Word about the new kid (along with my sister Karen and brother Joe) must have spread throughout the school like wildfire as we were suddenly thrust into the spotlight. Although my siblings had gained a much higher standard of knowledge and education, they would need to complete their Grade Twelve in order to get work, and so they had to attend school all over again. This country seemed ass backwards.

Suddenly I found myself surrounded by girls who wanted to hear me speak to them. Although I'd ask them to engage me in a conversation for sake of interaction, they would simply reply, "Just talk" from which I would lose interest. I'd point out they themselves had strong accents but they disagreed with my statement. On the other hand, guys would try to impersonate me but sounded ridiculous. In their own minds, while trying to be funny they thought they were the next best thing to sliced bread. In their ignorance, they'd tell me to speak English, learn how to talk properly or to get back on the boat I came from and go back to my own country in the mockery of my voice.

I found that the easiest way to shut them up was to ask where their family came from or if they were originally from Canada, which would define them as being "truly Canadian." I'd point out that unless they were Indigenous, they themselves were also immigrants. This left then in stunned silence, as their parents and grandparents had arrived on these shores from Europe or elsewhere and still spoke with an accent. My younger sister Angela went through much of the same at her school, but she assimilated very quickly into the dominant society and lost her brogue within a year of our arrival. It sure felt that life in this country was not offering much in the way of the welcoming I was told and was expected to believe. I lost interest in school, and didn't care much for whatever freedoms were supposedly associated to Canada. I sure as hell wasn't seeing or finding them outside of the insults and taunts from the guys.

At the end of classes and before the days of the Internet, I snuck into the computer room at school and used the phone that was set up for use with a modem. I'd called Elaine's house again for another 90 minutes. The principal was furious after getting a bill for this. I was in much deeper shite than the first time, as my parents got called to the school. The phones went into long-distance lockdown, and I was banned from ever using them again. At the time, no one understood how homesick I was and would do just about anything to get permanently kicked out. I almost succeeded in my efforts.

During the first Halloween dance I would ever attend, which was held at Churchill High School, I went out with a group of friends, who helped me purchase a twelve of beer. I drank nine of these within two hours behind an abandoned semi-trailer in a field north of Osborne Street and across from the transit garage in Fort Rouge. I hadn't eaten beforehand, so a fifteen-year-old who weighed 8½ stone at the time had a stomach full of beer.

I was completely blootered out of my skull and ready to take on the dance. That didn't last very long, so a mate who shares my first name and was out drinking with me decided the best course of action would be to take me somewhere to sober up. Good idea, but a bad mistake. I went totally ballistic. My homesickness had reached its first of many peaks, only to be fuelled by my alcohol intake.

I kicked an old rusty refrigerator frame in the back alley of Arnold Street just across from our school and immediately split my baseball boots and right foot wide open. Bleeding like a stuck pig and swearing at the destruction of my footwear, I cursed

Canada to no end for causing me this pain. In my mind, it would never have happened if I had been granted permission to avoid immigration.

Somehow, Greg managed to get my drunken arse over to Maria's house. Here they tried to settle me down with the help of a very well-built man by the name of Tony, who was a friend of theirs. They tried to restrain me but were not successful in their efforts. Unbeknownst to me though, Maria had child proofed her home since she and Larry had two young children. The mechanism did its job quite well but became my worst enemy. In my drunken stupor, I could not figure out how to escape. Every handle I grabbed had a protective device that prevented the door from being opened easily unless first squeezing the plastic cover.

Eventually Larry, Tony, and others managed to get me to my Aunt Maureen's house where she lived on Berwick Place. After getting me out of the car and onto the boulevard, I was still going ballistic and lashing out at everyone around me. My dad was brought out and tried to calm the situation to no avail. The last thing I remember hearing though is the words of my father as he stood squarely in front of me.

*"Son, this is going to hurt me a lot more than it will you..."*

WHAM. He wasn't kidding. His right fist connected squarely with the side of my face, dropping me instantaneously and laying me flat out on my back on the front lawn. He hadn't forgotten his naval training, but took measures into his hands in front of my family and the entire neighbourhood, who were now gathered on the front street due to my disturbance of the peace.

I ended up in St. Boniface hospital and received eight stitches. I was so intoxicated the doctor couldn't use anything to freeze the area, and so I felt every friggin' jab from the needle and thread sliding into the folds of my shredded skin in their efforts to piece me back together.

While in my drunken stupor, I had asked my uncle Malcolm to get money for me so I could permanently leave. He'd asked which bank I wanted, to which I responded "Any bank." Years later he informed me that he had taken $1,000 out so my wish could be realized. My parents never told me this, and I honestly don't fault them for it. There was really nothing for me to go back to, but it took eighteen years for me to realize this.

Although I struggled in trying to discover whatever Irish identity I had while trying to find my place in Canada, and through all the negative experiences I faced, there were more than enough positive moments that took years for me to appreciate. After five months of living in a much drier climate, I was pretty much cured of asthma and did not need to rely heavily on the daily doses of medications I had been taking since around the age of five.

Due to this newfound freedom from a lung ailment that had held me back for years, I found myself participating in sports beyond track and field. I began trying to understand the game of Canadian football. When not wandering the hallways, I would join many lads who became great friends and throw a ball around in front of the school grounds. Although, developing skills for the game and then trying to apply them on the gridiron are very different concepts! Since I had no idea what I was doing, and I was maybe 120 pounds soaking wet, I got knocked on my arse more times than I care to remember.

One thing I learned was to not curse under my breath in front of a coach, as they did not take that kind of language lightly. As a result of my behaviour, I was made to do countless crabwalk exercises up and down the embankment that ran alongside of Churchill Drive.

I was also given the chance to play basketball, and my mates always seemed amazed at how I could knock in a three-point shot so easily. All of the other skills necessary to play the game, such as dribbling or passing the ball, were not included in my athletic abilities, nor did I have the coordination needed to do these. I chose to go into the management end and let the guys with better skill sets do their thing.

The game I fell in love with and adopted as my own was team handball. Although we had a variation of handball back home played on the school grounds in an alley designed for one or two players, this was different. It required five players on a basketball-sized court as well as a goalie that protected a soccer-sized net.

I became captain of the "B" team as the "A" team was made up of players from the previous year. I gained this prestigious title due to my dedication to learn the sport *between* classes. I could constantly be seen running the hallways and practicing my three-point step, then flying though the air as if to take a shot on net. This was while the hallways were packed with other students, so I could pretend they were defenders from the other team. I would have to hone my skills to get past them.

I completely enjoyed and found my niche in team handball. Although I played as a right-winger, I did not wear protective wrist, elbow, or knee padding and ended up with more than my fair share of bruises. Our assistant coaches gave me the nickname Angus due to my mop of hair and uncanny ability to pull the same looks of the famous guitarist from AC/DC.

My science teacher—who was also my coach—had noted my efforts on more than one occasion. He mentioned this, along with a full re-enactment of my constant practice techniques, at our team wind up banquet after winning the provincial championships in 1988. Other teachers did not seem to have the same appreciation for me practicing these steps during the national anthem, as there was a policy that students were to stand completely still like statues whenever the song played. As I did not want to adhere to Canadian life and struggled to maintain my identity, I ignored their instruction and went about my way or refused to walk into school until the anthem had played so as to avoid it completely.

If I was not skipping classes or playing football in clear view of my teachers, I would be found at hotels in downtown Winnipeg meeting rock bands prior to their concerts. This was done with fellow headbanger and my good friend, Terry Lakusta. We appeared in a live broadcast of "Wild Side" by Mötley Crüe to thirty million viewers in Japan. This was filmed at the Teasers on Provencher Boulevard during their *Girls Girls Girls* World Tour.

It was the evening of Tuesday, October 20, 1987. Terry and I had finished working our shifts at a petrol station and had somehow gotten word that Crüe would be at Teasers later that night. At around one in the morning, Terry came over and picked me up at my parents' house and we headed out to the club. Nikki Sixx, Tommy Lee, and Mick Mars came out to sign autographs at around 5:00am before disappearing back into the club.

Within an hour of that, Tommy Lee came back out and stated, "If these fuckers aren't brought inside to join us, I'm not doing this shoot." The next thing we knew, Terry and I were being hustled inside with a bunch of other young lads to partake in Mötley Crüe's live video broadcast. I was only seventeen at the time, and this was my first time in such a place: both a bar and a strip joint.

We found our seats at a table that had a small wall separating us from the band by less than ten feet and in direct line of Tommy Lee. The experience was mind-blowing. Terry pumped his fists into the air while the shoot was taking place, and thought I should perhaps do the same thing, even though I did not think we were in the right place to be doing so. Whitesnake was in support on this tour, and it was fantastic to meet Adrian Vandenburg, Rudy Sarzo, and Tommy Aldridge later that day before the show that evening at the Winnipeg arena. For whatever reason, meeting bands always made their concerts that much more enjoyable and left a profound impact on us.

★★★★★

The last time I saw all of my friends from Belfast together yet separately was during my first trip home in 1992. It was the 8th of October when we got news that my granny had died from a massive heart attack. I told my mum and my aunt Maureen that I was going with them for the funeral, as we had all planned to reunite in 1993 but were never afforded the chance.

My mum had gone home in June of 1987 after her brother—my uncle James "Jimmy" Devlin—was tragically taken from us while in pursuit of one of his greatest passions in life: riding his ten-speed racer from Belfast to Dublin to meet up with the cyclists coming from that direction. She would not let me go home with her during that time as she knew she'd have never gotten me back to Canada at the conclusion of his funeral services.

When we arrived that morning and after walking through the door, my first thought was to see my granny lying in her coffin. In Irish tradition, we were to wake her. One person handed me a tin of Harp while another offered a cup of tea. At that very moment, food and drink was the last thing on my mind. Later in the evening, I drank eight bottles of cider. Compounded with the fact I hadn't slept for sixty-eight hours between booking flights, flying over, and going directly to a wake, didn't help my cause. I ended up getting my cousin Paul completely blitzed and in unfathomable shite with his ma when he went home that night, as the wake that was held for my granny was like no other.

Local musicians had stopped in with their instruments and before they began playing, they had a few drinks along with sampling platefuls of the countless meal choices that had been carefully prepared for everyone to enjoy. At one point, well after the music had begun playing and songs were sung by the masses in attendance, one of the musicians overheard someone saying to my aunt, "I'm very sorry to hear about the passing of your mum, Josephine." Flabbergasted, the musician turned to a dear friend of our family and said, "Mary. Is this a wake? Frig me. I thought this was a party for Josephine having her family home from Canada. This is the best wake I've ever attended." Obviously, my granny was receiving a phenomenal send-off.

The following evening while some nursed their hangovers and others continued to celebrate her life in what seemed to be a never-ending wake, the local priest came by to offer prayer. After saying a decat of the rosary, the priest asked who was doing the reading at the funeral? A gentleman who was sitting in the livingroom said he would do it and started laying down what he believed was his right.

I stood up and said, "Sorry, mate. I've no idea who you are, but do you see that wee lady in that coffin right there? That's my granny, and I was supposed to come home next year to visit with her. But I wasn't expecting to come home to this, so if you don't mind, I'll be doing a reading for her so I will." For whatever reason, people from Northern Ireland always end a sentence of with "so I will," "so I am," "so I had," or a combination thereof. For my granny's funeral, I chose the 23rd Psalm as my reading, so I did.

The very next day and in preparation for the service, I put on my Sunday best, which also happened to be the outfit I bought for my graduation from high school in 1988. I was still as skinny a wee frigger then as I was in 1992.

Upon approaching the altar, I reminded myself to genuflect before going up to the microphone (as I hadn't been in church for about five years at that point). I was extremely nervous – I knew I was going to be reading aloud to the congregation, and having only heard my brogue once before while doing an English assignment, I was thinking how dreadful it sounded. I somehow managed to get through it.

**How I looked in 1992. This photo was taken before I returned back home to Belfast for the first time.**

At the end of the service and after carrying my granny's coffin on our shoulders out to the awaiting hearse, quite a number of people—including Denis, other family who had heard I was home along with my mum and my aunt—came up to me and were completely shocked at how different I looked and had changed over the years. In their thick Belfast accents (which I was now hearing but had never noticed before) said, "Ack, Greg, you did a great job with that so you did, but for fuck's sakes will you please pick one language and stick to it?"

Before I could speak, my mum corrected us all. We were swearing like troopers. We apologized, and I thanked them but asked what they meant. The response was less than pleasing and burned into my brain. "Half that reading was Belfast, while the other half Canadian. You're a man of two countries and one without an identity. You need to get yourself sorted, mucker."

From being a fifteen-year-old kid when I left Belfast, immigrating to Canada and being told for years by the guys in Winnipeg to "slow down and speak proper English" or "get on your boat and go back to where you came from," to making every effort to lose my accent and assimilate into the dominant society so as to not get picked on, only to come back home as a twenty-two-year-old. The one difference being that I'd grown but was a complete stranger to two countries. I'd had enough. No longer was I going to take on an identity to please everyone else.

During the years we were away, in my mind life in Northern Ireland had stood still, completely frozen in time. I believed everyone was waiting for me to come home and pick up from where we left off. Seven years had passed, and although I had grown up and become a man in some ways (yet a child at heart in others), I honestly believed my mates would look exactly as I had remembered them. My mind had preserved them, hanging out in our old haunts and getting into the same childhood trouble while mucking about.

I believed "The Woodford Heavies," as my brother and his mates had so lovingly named themselves, would still be in existence.

My mates had stolen this title, along with the song they sung to acknowledge themselves as headbangers:

*It begins with a W and ends with an H,*
*With an F in the middle, W F H.*
*We are the Heavies from the Woodford Land.*
*We are the Woodford – Heavies!*

What a shock I received when I made my way back into Knockview. The SADOW field was no longer there – it was now filled with a new housing development. I cursed these houses and the people who lived in them, for they had destroyed one of our youth hangouts. They took away one of my most cherished and most hated childhood haunts.

This was where we played, rode motorbikes, snogged with our birds, drank, fought, and smoked. We would stay up half the night wandering the streets or played a game of hunts, in which a bunch of us would set out within a defined area, hide, then try to outrun our mates, who'd have to track us down. It was a basically a game of tag, but with our own twist.

We would meet in this field and use it as a shortcut or throw snowballs onto the Doagh Road from it. We'd have our bonefires here. Anything for a bit of fun, as there wasn't much else to do except go down by the waterfall in the forest and play a game we called "Stick the Knife." The essence of this game is that one of us would have to knick a butter knife from the cutlery drawer, take it into the forest, and set up a swing with a rope and part of a tree branch.

As we swung out over the small stream and while swinging backwards, we would try to stick the knife into the ground further back from wherever our mate had done so only moments earlier, or wrap it in behind a tree to make their next effort much more difficult, while watching them smack their heads in the process and laughing at their failed attempts.

Our youthful years were eradicated by construction. Elaine was getting married during this time, and Nicola asked if I wanted to go to the reception when I got home. We had stayed in contact for years by mail and telephone, but even that happiness would die over the years as our lives went in separate directions.

When I went home in 1992 after being away for seven years, this is what had become of the SADOW. My heart sank at this sight, as it was a clear destruction of my childhood memories.

My young friends had grown up and were moving full steam ahead down different paths. They no longer hung out together as one crowd and barely saw each other. They were now men and women living their own lives and doing their own things. My perfectly preserved memory was

The streets of Woodford Drive and Woodford Park that my mates and I used to muck around on have become a ghost town, compared to when they were filled with us all during the mid eighties.

completely shattered, for time had not stood still as I had thought it would. The precious memories and dreams from my youth that I had held so tightly onto for seven years were scattered upon my return home.

The last person I wrote to was Nicola. She had moved over to England for her job, and although we had kept in contact for years, I never received a final response from her. One of my longest pieces of correspondence to her was a fifty-four page handwritten letter along with thirty-six photographs. I would learn that she was settled into her career and had a well-defined British accent, completely different from what I knew and associated her with. She eventually got married and moved on in her life and career pursuits.

Everything I knew and longed for had eroded, and there was absolutely nothing I could do to change this. Yet I clung to those memories of years gone by while trying to block out the bitter portions, including the hatred that had started filtering into our neighbourhood from those who came from the council housing district that would question us before starting a fight. I felt so bloody cheated by this. As if I ever had control over it.

Over the years I was left with many questions but never received answers. What happened to my friends and our youth? The life I longed for was gone...

*Scattered Youth*

Recollecting my thoughts,
Of the years gone by.
Looking back to my childhood,
Heavy-breathed, I sigh.

I think of my friends,
And the places we played.
The secrets we kept,
The promises we made.

I reflect on the words,
To each other we'd say.
Tomorrow is our future,
Which now was yesterday.

With each morning that shone,
With every passing star.
Always there for one another,
We would never stray far.

Passing by along the street,
In our land of the Emerald Isle.
No matter our inner mood,
We managed to crack a smile.

Friendships were more than special,
We knew more than just a name.
Together we fought hard as one,
Never experiencing guilt or shame.

I thought our happiness would never end,
Through the days and years we'd seen.
Now fifteen years on down the line,
In a different country I've been.

Letters and calls once abundant,
Have all but come to a halt.
Should we say that being divided,
Is where we could lay fault?

We all have gone our separate ways,
New lives they have begun.
Anticipating one day we all reunite,
Before our final song is sung.

★★★★★

This is dedicated to the memory of my time with my many friends and countless others whom I have not mentioned. You know who you are.

Some of you I have seen in journeys home, including that during the first week of July in 2010 for a wedding of one of my most cherished friends, Rosie, who also happens to be the younger sister of Denis. Twenty-eight years away from you all now has made a huge difference in my life, but nothing can take away my childhood, which each and every one of you had a part in shaping.

Some rest in peace. My next-door neighbour Iain is just one of a few who have since passed in the years I've been away, but memories of our youth still live on within my heart and mind and will not be forgotten.

To some, our youth may be nothing more now than a distant memory. To me it is a part of my life that I will always cherish, growing up amongst you all as a Belfast child. Or, as some of you called me back then, "Reggie." I used this persona along with breakdancing or performing cartwheels in the middle of the street to try and bring a smile to your faces. Hatred and bitterness had started to make their ugly presence known within our once peaceful district. It was anything for a bit of craic and banter to offset the incoming shite.

I guess in some way it was a misspent youth, but it contained some of the happiest days of my life. In looking back now, it provided me with countless opportunities to define who I was, where I came from, and the pride I took from that. I had to discover that identity in a completely different country, since it wasn't allowed back home...

# Knockagh Monument

L ONG BEFORE I was born or my housing estate developed, a war memorial was erected and dedicated to the soldiers who died during the First World War from County Antrim. This is one of thirty-two counties in all of Ireland. There are six in the north and twenty-six in the south, along with four provinces named Ulster, Munster, Leinster, and Connacht. Ulster is made up of nine counties. Along with Antrim is Tyrone, Fermanagh, Down, Derry, and Armagh in the north, along with Cavan, Monaghan, and Donegal, although these are located in Southern Ireland.

This mighty memorial was re-dedicated in remembrance of those who hailed from County Antrim and lost their lives during the Second World War. It was built in 1936, stands at 110 feet, and is a replica of the Wellington Memorial located in Phoenix Park, Dublin. Its name is Knockagh Monument, and it imbedded its profound image into my young mind until the day I left.

The inscription on the base of Knockagh Monument acknowledges the services that were given during the Great War.

It seemed that Knockagh stood guard over our neighbourhood in Knockview. As far back as I can remember, while playing out in the garden with Karen, Joe, and Angela, we could simply look over and see this magnificent structure behind us while pondering what dark and haunting secrets it held. We would get ahold of our dad's binoculars and peer at this memorial with curiosity and awe, although

This is the view that I enjoyed for 15 years. In the distance is Belfast Lough, where we could watch the Sealink Ferry and oil tankers sail in and out daily. The far opposite shore is Bangor, Northern Ireland.

I never truly knew why it was there or what it meant. This was a symbol up on the mountain that looked out below to the permanently spoiled lands of "The Troubles" and the wars that raged for so long across Northern Ireland.

We were lucky for the most part, as the neighbourhood we grew up in was quite beautiful, with views behind our house of a lush green mountain rolling from left to right before dropping down out of sight; fields lined by hedgerows and filled with sheep or cows that roamed freely from the farmer, whose

Knockagh Monument as she stands in all of her glory.

property often left the stench of manure wafting across the valley and into our area. We would pinch our noses while complaining about the overpowering smell. But we were also lucky in that we were able to look directly into Belfast Lough from the top of our street and watch ferries come into port along with huge oil tankers. When coming home from school each day, this scenic view would capture our hearts and minds. I never really appreciated my surroundings until I left it all behind for the flatlands of the Manitoba prairies.

One day, Joe, who was always the adventurer, decided that it was time for us to go on our bikes and get a closer look. We must have been about eleven and thirteen years of age. The journey for two asthmatics would be grueling, as we were not physically trained to cycle up the mountainous roads, nor were our lungs capable of supporting us without bronchial inhalers due to the damp Irish climate that wrecked havoc on our chests.

We brought our dad's binoculars with us so once we reached our destination at the top of the mountain we would be able to have a bird's eye view of the landscape below, including Carrickfergus and the castle that stands on guard there. We spotted our mum working out the back of our house, washing windows and doing other chores. From up here she seemed to be much smaller than her 4'11" frame that towered over us.

Over the years and before leaving for Canada, friends from around our district would join us to make the difficult five-mile journey up to Knockagh. The awe of seeing this mighty

**A picturesque view as can be seen from Knockagh. Belfast Lough and the Cave Hill lie in the distance.**

structure has never left me. I find myself in a trance-like state every time I go home, only to see this impressive monument standing alone in the distance.

While home for Rosie's wedding, she asked if I would do one of the two readings on her special day. I was extremely delighted and honoured that she would ask me to do this. While having supper with her family, who I have always considered to be my second family as well, I read the scripture a few times to get comfortable with it. My heart was thumping with nervous anticipation, but I said it wouldn't be a problem.

The day arrived. I sat nervously in the pew and waited for the priest to give me the cue, as he had asked the first reader to come forth. However, this fellow ended up doing both readings, as the priest never called me. I guess this was partly my fault, since I hadn't stepped foot in a chapel for several years and completely missed my opportunity to try to read with one brogue, let alone two, as I had done at my granny's funeral several years before.

The day after the celebrations, which included meeting many old friends from our primary school days, Denis and I took my hired car up to Knockagh. We had last visited here when we were kids, yet here we now stood as adults. The experience was surreal to have us both standing there and looking at Newtownabbey below. It felt as if a passage in time was occurring, or that our lives had come full circle after being away for twenty-five years.

I'm dedicating this poem to my brother Joe McVicker, who brought me on a journey of intrigue to learn about the history of this monument. Thank you for the countless adventures that helped shape our childhoods over the years, Joe. The memories remain as strong and true within my mind today as they were on the days we created them, as if it were only yesterday.

### Knockagh Monument

For many a day,
And plenty of years.
You watched over my house,
Your shadow showed no fears.

Across the valley,
And up on the hill.
You stood there, so peaceful,
Incredibly still.

I would look out the window,
My eyes ablaze.
My focus entranced,
Feeling like I was dazed.

Like a soldier to attention,
You stood on your guard.
Looking out over Newtownabbey,
Surrounding fields so scarred.

Then the time, it did come,
One warm and sunny day.
My brother took my hand,
And he showed me the way.

So with this spellbound visit,
To the place we watched from afar.
My brother and I would venture,
Without the use of a car.

On our matching Choppers,
Our legs pedaled a pace.
We found the journey to be difficult,
With the wind caught in our face.

With our little hearts so eager,
Yet our wills determined, so strong.
We would come to face you,
Although the journey was quite long.

The narrow roads we followed,
Would take a twist or turn.
Because we cycled so hard,
Our muscles started to burn.

We would not stop very often,
Even to catch a breath.
Our curiosity kept us wanting,
To view the Memorial of Death.

When we reached the top of the hill,
Our journey almost complete,
We tasted the victory of a champion,
We would not smell defeat.

We embarked upon that final leg,
The road that tried to beat thee.
Now we would cheer in glorious shouts,
As we took ourselves to one knee.

With fire in our eyes,
Yet a passionate stare.
We focused on your might,
As bold as we did dare.

We read the names of,
The people who were so brave.
They put down their lives in world wars,
Sending their courage to an early grave.

Now in your shadow we stand tall,
And still we show no fear.
For now we know the purpose,
Of why you have been placed here.

We looked out across the valley,
To the house where we play ball.
It's funny now seeing you incredibly huge,
And our grand home so small.

For when we look at you each day,
You look not so big in might,
We can close you between our fingers,
And knock view out of sight.

Now that we have had the chance,
Standing upon your sacred ground.
We know that we can be rest assured,
You'll gaze at us year round.

## Stranger To My Land

GROWING UP IN Belfast was very difficult, although it seemed completely normal at the time. I dare ask if someone could please explain what is normal about being awoken in the middle of the night by their mother at the age of six to prevent my siblings and me from being scarred permanently by a pending blast twenty-five yards from our house? A bomb had been planted in the back of a shopkeeper's vehicle. This is just one of many experiences we faced associated with "The Troubles." In hindsight, this helped me understand why my parents would not let me know that my uncle Malcolm had secured $1,000 to send me home in 1985 after my drunken experience at the Halloween dance.

I was called a Fenian bastard (Feen Yun), the son of a Fenian whore and other slanderous terms because I was raised as an Irish Roman Catholic living on the land of my ancestors. How I became labeled with this derogative term is still unbeknownst to me. A Fenian was an Irish soldier who fought in the Battle of the Boyne in 1690, at least 280 years before my birth.

It took me several years to appreciate why I was held at a security checkpoint in 1979 at a swimming baths. Upon entering the area, my cheeky eight-year-old self announced to the staff, "There's nothing to worry about. There's only a bomb in my bag." I honestly did not comprehend the impact of my statement, as I thought I was just joking with them. What I did not understand however was that such comments were not taken lightly whatsoever. Due to the protection of our young minds as was given by my mum in her efforts to shield us from "The Troubles," I did not immediately grasp the implications of what I had just said, but the severity of making such a stupid statement was quickly brought to fruition.

As a result of my cheek, stupidity, and lack of comprehension of our surrounding environment, the entire student body was allowed to go on to the swimmers, while I was made to feel like a complete idiot at the hands of the security staff (which they had every right to do). They held my bag back, and as they searched through it, they emptied the contents onto the table. A towel and a change of underclothing spilled out of it. The staff proceeded to made fun of the pattern on my matching tops and bottoms. They did this in front of our principal and the worst teacher I had ever known during my primary school years, which did not make things easier for me. She loved my brother to bits but completely despised me. Her hatred for me still lies deep within me, as does the bark of her voice. I never understood why her black leather strap, which was embedded with metal studs and used to take layers of skin from my hands, was named after my dad. I paid a price at the end of this weapon for my stupid comment once we got back to our school, and learned another severe lesson upon my arrival home.

While going with Joe or Denis for day trips during our school holidays, it took years of me living away from Belfast to understand why a bus conductor would walk to the back where we sat and ask us to get up from our seats before pulling the cushions off and looking into the cavities below. They were checking to see if a device had been planted. In all those years and bus trips along the Antrim Road, where we could look through the windows over to Bellvue Zoo, which lay peacefully on the slope of the mountain beneath the watchful eyes of the Cave Hill; or into Belfast Lough to the Harland and Wolff shipyard, where the Titanic was built and prior to her maiden voyage of death on April 15, 1912, that we ourselves were possibly sitting on top of a bomb. Yet we took this as a natural occurrence and thought nothing of it. My mum had always warned us to not kick empty tins in the street in case they were booby-trapped.

In 1981, one of the most terrifying incidents we faced as children occurred well after I made my poor choice of words while walking into the swimming baths. My dad was home from sea on one of his limited leaves of absence. During this time, my cousin Treasaigh had moved back to Belfast and was living around the corner from us, along with her mum and dad, my aunt Maureen and uncle Malcolm.

My dad decided to take Treasaigh, Karen, Joe, and I to see a James Bond movie called *For Your Eyes Only*. Angela stayed home with my mum, as she was only six-years-old. As we sat with our sweets in hand, and watched our favourite action hero do his best to fend off the bad guys on a snow covered ski slope, a car bomb exploded outside the ABC theatre on Great Victoria Street. This was either timed to go off at the same time as the explosion that occurred during the movie, or someone in the audience or the projection booth had a detonator in his or her hand. My dad believed that the most bombed hotel in all of the United Kingdom was once again targeted: The Europa.

We were on the upper level balcony, and as the building shook from the shockwave created by the bombing, we screamed. In our state of panic, we tried to get up and run, along with every other patron caught in this explosion. My dad threw his body over the four of us with his arms and legs fully outstretched, pinning us to the seats while saying, "Stay down and don't move. You don't go outside, as there might be a second one waiting for you." What he was referencing is that once the first explosion had gone off and had created its intended shock, panic, and chaos, a second device was usually planted and packed with glass, barbed wire, nails, and shrapnel, to cause as much human devastation as possible.

During my trip home in 2010 for Rosie's wedding, I was saddened to see that the hatred I grew up with continued long after the Peace Agreement was signed on March 26, 1997. I was sickened to see that flags of hatred were once again fastened to every lamppost. What was more ghastly is that the fires used to celebrate the eleventh night were already well in preparation.

I asked myself—after 3,700 lives had been lost as a result of "The Troubles," why preparations continued to recognize these events that only induce more hate? Nothing has ever been solved by them, and it leaves the world sickened by the sectarian riots that unfold thereafter. What was even more shocking is that a statement was released saying that tourists from around the world flock to Northern Ireland to participate in the twelfth celebration. That is like saying people should flock to Syria or Egypt to be a part of the political uprising the world is seeing right now in those nations, or should take a holiday over to join the child soldiers in Sierra Leone. Nothing could be further from the truth. This led me to ask if those within the political structure of Northern Ireland have their heads firmly imbedded?

I have many friends who come from both sides of the community and who have no use or interest in whatever is sought from these hate-fuelled proceedings and the divide they cause. They pack up during this time to escape all the associated rubbish. Sectarian oppression and violence are never justifiable as acceptable practice, for they are human rights violations. Will you ever learn? Sadly, I do not believe that will ever happen in this generation or the next.

## Stranger to my Land

In my beloved town of Belfast,
Off goes yet another devastating bomb blast.
In the streets the people lie dying,
Over their bodies, their families start crying.

In a land that is run by hatred and rule,
Fragile people are made to feel like a fool.
Where the citizen's would like to have the choice,
Freedom of speech, the language in their voice.

Both sides, for their marches and silly parades,
Look like nothing more than a game of charades.
While they walk so defiant, they chant and they shout,
"Soon we will get all of those other bastards out."

While we know the place is well overrun,
By ignorance, who shall hide behind a gun.
They target all innocence that lock into sight,
They continue their torture by day and by night.

When people do apply for a job,
Noses are turned up just like a snob.
"We will only hire from our own kind,
You're fully qualified, but not what we had in mind."

There are many armies that walk the street,
They point their guns at certain people they meet.
They know whose side that they will take,
Their sincerity can be determined as nothing but fake.

To the people that live on the non-sectarian road,
When they ask for assistance, they are left in the cold.
The safeguards that were put into place,
Will shower them with bullets and spit in their face.

I wonder if my country will try and make peace,
Will the guns stay silent? Will the violence cease?
Will people no longer hide behind a frown?
Will they finally have freedom from the bitterness they drown?

My closing word to the nations of the Emerald Isle:
Hold your heads high, and be proud when you smile.
Now is the time for the healing seeds to grow,
Give a chance to be united, and not for what you know.

# Hallows' Eve

THE NORTH AMERICAN experience of Halloween is extremely different compared to that of Northern Ireland. One day and while discussing this yearly event with a colleague, Siobhán, along with the different terminologies we use to describe clothing, it left me thinking that perhaps the Irish were backwards. I had shared that my neighbour and I would use an anorak—a parka that has a hood lined with fake fur—as part of our costume. I then suggested that a hoodie could be used to create the same effect. Siobhán described this as being a "Bunny Hug" in her birthplace, where their biggest pride is the football team, the Saskatchewan Roughriders. The "Riders" won the 101st Grey Cup this year at home in front of their adoring followers.

Their fans are second to none and have shown the rest of the country what team pride is all about. The "Rider Nation" faithful dress up like their favourite players, make helmets out of watermelons, paint their faces green and white, and create costumes out of every piece of Roughrider merchandise they can get their hands on. They travel en mass to other cities and party with the home team fans before the game by having a barbeque and a few drinks together in the carpark, before continuing their celebrations in the stands with friendly banter. Since they do this during the entire season, it would seem that Halloween occurs every game day throughout the pre, regular, and post season of football in this Canadian province. Go Riders! Sadly, this is in stark contrast as compared to the violence that is sickeningly created by soccer hooligans back home, who are hell-bent on inflicting physical injury onto fans from opposing teams and are kept on separate sides of the stadium.

I first saw the differences in how we celebrate this ritual back home to that of Canada, when my daughter Caitlin was a wee tote walking through a mall wearing a bumblebee costume. She would go from store-to-store carrying her pumpkin-shaped bucket, watching closely as shop vendors dropped sweets into the pail. It would swing from her hand while people said, "Awww." It makes a parent feel proud to see and hear this in response to their children.

Moving from the mall, in the following year, I took her from door-to-door within our snowy neighbourhood. I would walk up the pathway with her, and upon our arrival I would recite the words, "Trick or treat." When the homeowner answered, Caitlin would say in the softest voice, "Twick or tweet... pwease," which was followed up by, "Thank you" after receiving her lollipop, a small packet of crisps, or chocolate bar.

Caitlin, ten months of age and almost ready to celebrate her first Halloween as a bumblebee. She also had a wee hat made with black pipe cleaner antennas.

In our enclave of Knockview, my neighbour Iain and I would go out door-to-door but we didn't ask for tricks or treats. Instead, we had to sing a song to the person who answered the door that went like this:

*Halloween is coming round, and the goose is getting fat,*
*Would you please put a penny in the old man's hat?*
*If you haven't got a penny, a ha'penny will do,*
*If haven't got a ha'penny, God Bless you and your old man too.*

We used to have half pennies in our currency, and would be overjoyed when we would find them discarded on the streets, as we could buy a mojo or a blackjack (soft chewy sweets about the size of a thumb nail and tasted like fruit salad or liquorice). The simple pleasures we used to enjoy.

Iain and I would take turns putting our anoraks on backwards and have the other zip it up from behind, covering our face, body, and head. The one who was wearing his anorak properly would leave it unzipped at the neck area so his face was fully showing. We had our methodology down pat. As we walked up the pathways before we rapped the door or rang the bell, the one who had his face fully covered would stand upright and take the other by the head, trying to hide as much as his body as possible.

We hoped that when the homeowner answered he or she would see a headless horseman, although we did not have a horse to accompany us. We thought our gimmick was brilliant and deserved a gold medal. Others, however, and specifically the homeowner (whose time we were obviously wasting) told us we were too cheap to buy a plastic Halloween mask at the Woodford shops for 10p.

Ciarán, who loves Halloween, decided to be a Clone Trooper from Star Wars. He was around five years of age here.

Their assumptions were very much correct, as we were often met with, "Ack, wee lads, will ye take yerselves off by the hawn and quit wastin' my time for flips sake."

After countless doors were closed in our faces, Iain and I were determined to not come away empty handed. We would mutter all sorts of nasty names under our collective breaths about the individual who answered the door for not crossing our palms with silver or a bloody ha'penny for that matter.

We walked home and went our separate ways. My mum would have hot custard and cake waiting, along with apples in a bucket so that my siblings and I could bob for them. We never did learn from our previous experiences, as every year we'd end up swallowing a mouthful of water and half-drowning ourselves in the process.

My mum would have a packet of sparklers for us, which we would light; then we would run around our back garden, sticking them between the fir trees and half hoping they would catch on fire. In hindsight, part of our wishes did come true, as we would roast our fingertips and get them subsequently blistered by touching the wrong end of the scorching metal after the sparks stopped flying every which direction.

I understand that communities across Northern Ireland now follow the North American custom of trick or treat and hand out sweets rather than having two wee lads come to their doors making complete eejits of themselves while seeking a few pennies. Although I went home in 1998 and called around to see my neighbour's family as I always do, they weren't home.

Sadly, in 1999 I would learn he was tragically killed in a motorbike accident not far from our house. I never did get to look back on our childhood days with him, except while I was standing at the foot of his grave in 2003 on yet another trip home.

Thus, this reflection and poem are dedicated to your memory, Iain. Rest in peace, my friend, and thank you for this chance to reflect on our childhoods. I know I will see you again someday, and we'll laugh at how much fun we had every year on October 31st.

## Hallows' Eve

The leaves, they all have fallen,
Final destination is the ground.
As the wind breezes through so gently,
The decay jumps to life with sound.

Darkness has cloaked the earth,
Yet no child will show a frown.
For this moment, it's not time for bed,
Instead they'll awaken the town.

The pumpkins are all carved,
Eagerly waiting to be lit.
Boldly taking their lifeless places,
On the porchways where they sit.

Witches pass by shrieking,
Ghosts, they whisper boo.
Doing the very best they can,
To frighten the life right out of you.

The children are all in costume,
Their hands wishing for a treat.
Along the path to every house,
They shuffle their anxious feet.

When they reach the doorway,
The moon is shining through.
Make sure that you fill every bag,
Or they might play a trick on you.

Listen to the neighbourhood,
And the laughter that fills the air.
"Trick or treat" surprises you quick,
It's a two-foot grizzly bear.

Celebrating the ritual of Hallows' Eve,
Illuminated by moonlight.
Children of all shapes and sizes,
Will appear at your door tonight.

As this evening draws to a close,
The zombies have gone back to their tomb.
Take a glance towards the night sky,
And capture a witch flying out on her broom.

# The Socialization of Hate

I HAD ACCOMPANIED my then six-year-old son to his pediatrician's office. While waiting for our name to be called, I watched in silent awe as children played together. In this office were children from various ethnic and cultural backgrounds, but no one pointed this out. There was no racial divide. They did not say how they differed from one another due to skin colour, nor did they ask each other what their religion was.

I found myself looking back at where I grew up and reflected upon the origins of the socialization of hate. For years I was asked what foot I kicked with, if I supported the Pope or the Queen, how I recited the Our Father, if I knew "The Sash My Father Wore," how I said my alphabet, what football team I followed, or if I was green or orange. All of these terms were used as a product of hate, and to find out whether one was Catholic or Protestant. What did it matter? We were growing up in a country with people from other nationalities who immigrated to Northern Ireland. These were people from the white, black, and yellow races. But again, race is a socially constructed term, so why did any of this matter?

Growing up in the eighties, I was often involved in collecting material to use for the twelfth bonfire. The Protestant majority has celebrated the twelfth of July for over three hundred years, recounting the Battle of the Boyne, which took place in 1690 between King James II and King William of Orange III.

At midnight every July 11, we would burn the stacked pile of collected materials we had stored in the SADOW field. But lighting the fire was not to be done by an Irish Catholic, nor should they have ever been in attendance. People from my peaceful neighbourhood would emerge drinking alcohol and speaking about Fenian bastards, cheers erupting when an effigy of the Pope was recklessly tossed onto the fire to burn.

Children from the neighbourhood witnessed these events and learned hatred that very night, as well as during the practice marches in preparation for the twelfth day. Those who were not Protestant learned to hate themselves or call out against their own kind in order to protect themselves while in attendance of such fires.

Curbs would be painted red, white, and blue, signifying the Union Jack. Young boys, having taken the handle from their mothers' brooms, would tape these same three colours along the handle. After adding a tennis ball to the top to make a baton, they began their practice by swinging this around their neck, twirling it and throwing it high into the air as they led their parade battalion forth along with their songs of hatred.

I reflected upon seeing youngsters no older than five years of age dressed in their best Sunday suits, parading alongside of their fathers and wearing orange sashes. These children were taught what hatred for another human is all about: anyone who was a Catholic was a Fenian and not to be associated with. The innocence connected to their young minds was quickly fractured and removed.

Returning eighteen years later, I was shocked to see this practice continued. While traveling from Belfast to Scotland by ship, I walked through the duty free area. I watched a seven-year-old boy put a jester's hat on his head with the colours green, white, and orange, which resembled the Irish flag. His sister, maybe ten years of age, shouted at her brother, "Get that Fenian crap off before da sees you and knocks your head in."

Needless to say I was ashamed that socialized hatred through colour schemes still continued all these years later, and that green, white, and orange automatically makes one inferior, whereas red, white, and blue deemed another as superior. These colour schemes determined acceptance, social standing, religious, and political views.

Snapping out of my moment of reflection, the youngsters continued to play together and did not disassociate from others. Their innocence was intact, waiting to be shattered by biases presented today within the larger society in which they live, grow, and play.

We can learn a lot from children. We can learn how to interact with one another and not hate other individuals because of their cultural background, race, or skin colour. We can learn that if we work together in peace for the same goals, we are able to accomplish so much more. We can learn that being human does not mean oppressing someone else for our own benefit and gain, but that we can all be equal. As adults we sometimes feel we have all the answers. Maybe it is time we listen and learn from our children, as they may hold the key to ending discrimination, racism, and socialized hatred.

# The Confessional

WHEN I MADE my First Holy Communion at eight years of age, I was taken all around my relatives' houses and presented in my Sunday best with a big blue ribbon attached to the lapel of my blazer. This made it look like I had won first prize in a beauty contest or was a trophy from the racetrack. However, upon arriving at my aunt Josephine's house she said, "C'mere son. Here's a few bob in your pocket." I never understood who bob was or why she wanted him in my pocket. It meant I got a few quid to spend. In my opinion, it was compensation for being paraded around and having to go through the trauma associated with this day. I was following a system that in order to be welcomed into God's home, I needed to undergo this rite of passage.

In adulthood, I began asking what this planet would look like if all the destruction, greed, and devastation that occur due to the selfishness of others were to end and we all lived as equals. So how is it then that we are damned to all salvation for eternity by not practicing or believing in faith-based systems such as Christianity? The world has now seen the devastating actions and effects caused by pedophile priests and Christian brothers. I've borne witness to these behaviours while attending secondary school, thus the reason for the almost complete destruction of my use of Gaeilge, which is also known as Gaelic.

This language was completely foreign to me, as I only began learning it at age twelve. It was not recognized by the British school boards and was not taught to us. I was often told it was a dead language or that no one used it except for Fenian bastards sympathetic to dissident republicans, fighting for their independence from the Crown.

In 1980 while across the border in the Republic of Ireland, the Free State, or the Emerald Isle (which are just some of the names associated to the south), I found it strange that Gaeilge took precedence over English and was part of radio and television programs, but was also spoken fluently by people who resided there. So much for it supposedly being a dead language. Dead by definition, influence, destructive beliefs and patterns of hatred against other humans, as was seen for many years throughout the north of Ireland.

Prior to attending secondary school, a friend of mine who had just completed his first year told me to watch out for a certain Christian brother. He gave me his name and, to directly quote him from that day, said the brother in question "is a friggin' fruit."

Sure enough, when attending my first year of class, I watched more than enough times as young men around my age were fondled, groped, sexually violated, and exploited on a repeated basis while we were supposed to be learning our mother tongue. The name given to the brother should have been that of "a friggin' pedophile," as that is exactly what he was, preying on the flesh of young and unsuspecting boys.

After posing a question in Gaeilge such as, "An bhfuil cead agam a ghabháil chun an leithris, le do thoil?" which translates into "May I go to the bathroom, if you please?" the pedophile had no problem asking his pupils in his "gentle" voice to "come closer, come closer." He would allow his hands to caress their backs down to their backside and give a soft squeeze.

On occasion, he would also ask me to do the same for him, to "come closer," but I would keep my distance and respond in English, "I've already asked my question. Am I free to go?" I was determined to not become an unwilling participant or be violated to help satisfy his sexual craving for boys while hiding behind the lies of his plastic white collar.

This perverse fucker would always add a smile and pathetic laugh when fondling his students, almost a sign of his own self-assurance when having them become a part of his disgusting ways. His voice was never soft though when my classmates and I would spell a word and forgot to add the fada, which is the accent as noted above: the second "a" in the word "ghabháil." He'd be eating an apple, his face furious as if the devil was speaking from within him. Bits of the peel were spat all over his desk as he screamed at the top of his lungs, "DON'T FORGET YOUR FUCKING FADAS," as he slammed his leather strap down on the desk.

The strap was another one of his favourite instruments and an extension of himself. This was not only used to leave us with stinging hands, but also for shoving under the desk and between the legs of his students, trying to stimulate any boy he felt worthy of being on the receiving end of his foul, disgusting, nauseating actions. It sickens me now, as I can clearly see him in my mind with his perfectly pressed black trousers and polished shoes, his dandruff-laden blazer and a deep blue shirt, with his white hair, rimmed glasses, and the snide smirk that preceded his violation of my classmates.

I remember many a desk being pushed back, including mine under my own weight to avoid being violated by this hot-tempered predator. We learned to not sit in the front row, but it did not deter his sexual intentions and cravings for us. We were not safe, but were left to watch a grown man rub the crotch of his pants, gloating in his self-serving splendor of pleasure.

We were given the opportunity to go to the Gaeltacht, where we would participate in six weeks of Irish lessons while taking in events such as horseback riding, fishing, rock climbing, and other outdoor sports. But I never took the school or the brother up on their offer. If learning the Irish language and what might have been my mother tongue was associated with personal buggery beyond the classroom by some repugnant monster, I was definitely not interested.

I have no idea what happened to this brother after my first year of secondary school, as I went on to have other Gaeilge teachers, but the actions of this pedophile destroyed my trust in the Irish language. What is more sickening than this is that when I was home in 2010, twenty-five years after leaving, I learned from one of my mates that his younger sibling attended the same school long after I left, probably about seven or eight years later. The same actions occurred during his years in school.

The school board and Roman Catholic Church were fully aware of what was happening. This should not be a surprise to anyone with all of the recent disclosures that came out of Ireland in Christian-run schools, churches, and orphanages, but also in St. John's, Newfoundland. The movie called *The Boys of St. Vincent* captured brutalities and grotesque events similar and worse to that of what we experienced. This abuse has also been well documented in other societies and cultures across the globe, but it does not provide solace to know we were not the only ones exposed to this atrocious behaviour and the decimation of our childhoods.

I'm sure there'll be many more disclosures in the coming years, but there will also be a lot of silence, since people do not wish to relive trauma associated with childhood sexual victimization. This scar permeates communities and individuals within every facet of society. Simply throwing compensation at the damage does not eradicate the painful memories or the destruction of children's very identities.

I have to ask this: what if we did not have to hide our shame due to the sick and completely vile actions of someone who protects themselves under the watchful eyes of God while cowering behind a white collar? And what if learning a traditional, although foreign voice within the land of our ancestors was taught by priests and brothers who did not abuse their power by fondling and molesting their pupils? Would we be proud in knowing our mother tongue fully?

*Mo chara, tirgan teanga, tirgan anam!*
*My friend, a country without language, is a country without soul!*

I have since listened to hundreds of heartbreaking and gut-wrenching stories of Indigenous people in Canada and how they are still trying to comprehend why they were chosen to be unwilling participants for priests, nuns, and educators within the Indian Residential School system for deeds of sexual gratification. When disclosing this abuse they were hushed or smacked, as it was considered sinful to speak out against a person considered to be closer to a higher being.

I do not wish to dedicate this composition to anyone and certainly not to the abusers such as the brother who taught in the school I attended, and who passed himself as being seated at the right hand of God as defined through Christian ideology.

This composition is not intended to be a saving grace for those who found themselves on the receiving end of these actions. The memories you have had to endure at the hands of these pedophiles are quite painful and may require a lifetime of healing, which some of you may never find. Rather, my intention is to try to bring to light the disgraceful and secretive deeds that went on behind closed doors in schools run by such individuals across many nations, which have destroyed countless souls, lives, and families. There is no gratification in rape except for the rapist. It is an act of power and control. It is an act of human degradation.

I no longer follow Christian-based practices, but instead respect my teachings from my own appreciation of a higher being, whether I choose to say Creator, Great Spirit, or God. Religion was beaten into me. My spirit comes from within my soul. One simply does not replace the other.

Two questions remain. Do priests and Christian brothers who utilize pedophilic practices believe their sins are forgiven after confessing them? Since they proclaim to be messengers of God, are they granted clemency? Perhaps, or at least until the next time they assault, violate, or sexually exploit yet another unsuspecting child.

## The Confessional

In the name of the Father,
And of the Son,
Dear God, forgive me,
For the sins I have done.

Although not a priest,
But a Christian brother.
Behind my rosary,
I place my cover.

I covet my pupils,
Allow them no choice.
With the Celtic language,
I teach them their voice.

They are my boys,
I love them so dear.
When they speak to me,
I respond, "Come here."

My hands they wander,
To capture a feel.
Those pretty young boys,
I ask them to kneel.

Look up at me, child,
For I want you to know.
Open your mouth wide,
My seed I will sow.

Once I am done,
Wipe your lips dry.
Keep this our secret,
My child, do not cry.

God will bless you,
For this deed you have done.
You're free to go,
Thank you, my son.

Who will be next?
In front of my chair.
Praise to you, Lord,
Hear my prayer.

## An Ode to My Aunt Sadie

I HAD ONLY GOTTEN to know my aunt Sadie upon coming to Canada. Along with my uncle John and just like my own parents had done, she wanted to afford her children a greater opportunity to prosper. In the late sixties and early seventies at the beginning of "The Troubles," they left Northern Ireland and immigrated to Winnipeg. Her accent was as strong as the day she left.

We tragically lost her one night in the 1990s. Upon going to the funeral home, we were all offered the opportunity to get up and say a few words. As anyone who has attended a funeral service can attest to, it takes an awful lot of strength and courage to get up in front of a crowd while trying to put emotions in check and speak words of wisdom about the person we loved. My mum did just this as I sat in silence, carefully listening to her words, spoken so eloquently.

My aunt always had the most brilliant way of saying "Oh frig," the use of which I was constantly scolded for in Winnipeg, as it was supposedly a swear word. She loved the song "Spirit In The Sky" as originally recorded in 1969 by Norman Greenbaum, but the version we all came to appreciate was the re-release in 1986 by Doctor and the Medics.

In following the tradition of many an Irish family, my cousins planned a get-together after the funeral and had a celebration for my aunt's life. Prior to going I had decided to try my hand at eulogizing her. I listened as my mum told me about how my aunt and uncle got together and what they did to ensure their happiness against the wishes of many. I captured those words and shared them with my cousins who were present.

As sad as a funeral can be with the passing of a family member, a composition like this can be used to reflect upon memories of happiness. It is truly a great way to begin the healing journey.

### An Ode to my Aunt Sadie

Sarah Anne Corbett was once a wee woman,
Who came from the land of the green.
Along came my Uncle John,
And she became his beauty queen.

Off to England, they did run,
And husband & wife they became.
Although some gave not their blessing,
They married all the same.

That magical day they did elope,
Must have been a match made in heaven.
For only a handful of people knew,
That she was now called Sadie Devlin.

Their love for each other grew stronger each day,
And five young children would appear.
John, Sarah, Maria, Jim, and the saintly one, Patrick,
Their ages each separated by a year.

From Belfast to Canada, the family did come,
And a new life it would start.
My wee Auntie Sadie,
Loved Uncle John with all her heart.

My wee auntie Sadie had quite the Irish brogue,
And another thing I'll tell ya, her heart was made of gold.
Her kindness, compassion, her love and forgiveness,
Would never ever turn cold.

The warmth in her smile, the gleam in her eyes,
The way she said, "Oh Frig."
My wee auntie Sadie always did prefer a headbang,
Over a good wee Irish jig.

Aunt Sadie's favourite song,
Was "Spirit In The Sky."
And with that spirit she now is with,
That no one can deny.

So to my wee aunt Sadie,
Here's to us and "frig" the rest.
It definitely is a blessing to know,
You are one of the very best!

With love for you in your new life with Uncle John,
And for all of those who have gone before us.

★★★★★

On the morning of October 25, 2013, word had rippled throughout our family circle that an unfortunate and tragic accident had claimed the life of my cousin, Jim Devlin. He was forty-seven years young when he was taken from us. A few months prior to his death and after attending a hockey game with my son, Ciarán, we were lucky enough to bump into Jim and his lovely wife, Rachel, who was also a dear friend of mine from our years together in Churchill High School. This gentle giant surprised me when he said, "Hey cousin. How are you doing?"

As Jim was a staunch supporter of the Boston Bruins, I chuckled as he bantered with Ciarán, who was wearing a Los Angeles Kings hat. Sadly, this was the last time we would see Jim.

I have often said to my cousin, Sarah, that although we are like many others around this world who are connected to one another through social media, it brings to light the importance of seeing and regularly spending time with family, cousins, and friends, or staying in contact with each other outside of chance meetings. As was the case with this mournful occasion, we all came together for yet another family funeral. Since we never know what life has in store for us from one second to the next, it is so important to live life to the fullest and for what it brings today, as tomorrow is never guaranteed.

As you know Jim, your service was extremely beautiful. The hundreds that were in attendance, and those who fought back tears while they spoke, exemplified the true testament of your character and how proud you were of your Irish heritage. It goes without say that you will be sorely missed by all who knew and loved you. Your passing has left a huge void in the hearts of several community organizations in and around Fort Rouge, a place that you've called home since arriving here in 1970. Give my love to all our family. Rest in peace, cousin.

Whispers in the Breeze

MANY OF US have had to deal with the uncertainty of death. The coping mechanisms used to get through this difficult period can be short or last for many years, depending on our individual mannerisms and how we look back on the person's life.

Death at any age is difficult no matter how we try to frame it. We may find ourselves saying, "They lived a long and meaningful life" or "what a terrible shame to die at such a young age." This is one way of trying to come to terms with their passing, which of course is a natural cycle in life.

Some say time heals all wounds. Perhaps, but when one opens a photo album or picks up a gift from their beloved, memories come flooding back and the grieving begins all over again. In some cases, this can become a lifelong process.

Take a moment and ask how many times you've opened a paper to read the obituaries? Who they are? Where did they live? What did they do or accomplish? Those they've left behind. I recall my friend Kevin telling me that he reads the obituaries every day. As he explained, this was his way of showing respect for that person's life. The ritual that begins thereafter every year includes an "In Memoriam" in which we see a tribute, poem, or a reflection of what that person meant to their family in life and how badly they are missed.

I went through this process myself upon visiting my granny and granda's graves. I never really knew my granda, as he died nine months after I was born. My granny on the other hand was a steady fixture in our lives. We spent a lot of time visiting her in Belfast as well as when she moved within a ten-minute walk from where we lived.

Lost in a trance that day as I gazed at their headstone, it suddenly dawned on me I was following a process that many others do. People from all around this world, regardless of age, race, culture, or religious background, enter into the same processes and reflect upon the lives of their beloved family members. There I stood in a lonely graveyard, reminiscing on the lives once shared before their untimely passing.

Untimely as defined within our own minds, as we find ourselves wishing that we could have spent more time with them before their death. Things we wanted to say in life but never found the time to. Things we now want them to know or things that we should never have said in the first place. I found myself asking my grandparents for their guidance and prayers from beyond the clouds that day.

While looking out towards Belfast Lough, my daughter Caitlin, who was four-years-old at the time, stood close by yet did not fully comprehend that her great-grandparents lay in the graves beneath our feet.

I took this picture at the foot of my granny and granda's graves, looking out towards Belfast Lough. I composed "Whispers in the Breeze" while standing here in 1998 when I was home visiting for only my second time since leaving Belfast in 1985.

I reflected that my life began because my grandparents gave birth to my mum. I reflected on their passing. I realized one-day my loved ones and my children would be doing the same thing I was doing at that very moment while standing at the foot of *my* grave. Pausing to reflect.

Our lives are simply fleeting glimpses of time, as we never know when our journey ends or a new one begins.

## Whispers in the Breeze

Realizing my innermost fears,
Choking back the steady stream of tears.
Not knowing your time had come,
Without you I feel so numb.

Just a whisper in the breeze,
Brought my world down to its knees.
The day that you were called away,
Paradise is where you now stay.

When the days do come to pass,
I call upon your bed of grass.
Comfort inside knowing you're there,
Looking up at my vacant stare.

The silence I exchange with thee,
Speaks volumes, I'm sure this you'll see.
My shadow casts across your grave,
While I stand so lonely, I stand so brave.

Now the days they seem so long,
In your arms is where I belong.
I close my eyes and hear you speak,
You call my name; my legs feel weak.

Together we promised that we would grow old,
We thought our happiness would never unfold.
I kneel at your feet with my head hung low,
Thoughts in my mind you already know.

This quality time with you I spend,
Will hopefully help my broken heart mend.
Feeling guilty when I turn to leave,
Returning home I continue to grieve.

When my term approaches death,
Time to exhale one final breath.
I wonder if others will fall to their knees,
When my name whispers in the breeze.

# The Enchantment of Achill

NESTLED IN THE heart of Country Mayo, is a place called Achill Island. Achill is the largest island that lies off the west coast of Ireland, but it is connected to the mainland by a bridge. My first and regrettably only time here occurred

This signpost can be seen when first coming into Achill Island.

in 1998. I longed to get there again to find myself lost not only in the tranquility of the beautiful landscape itself, but to be once again encompassed by the haunting energies that surround that part of my homeland.

A quick search on the Internet will show any viewer the beautiful scenery that Achill has to offer. Hidden within the land are some of the darkest secrets of the 1840s and for centuries long before that, buried among the ruins found at the Deserted Village

This is the breathtaking scenery that is seen looking out from the Deserted Village at Slievemore. Ruins from abandoned homes dot the landscape.

at Slievemore. Spending a day here to explore these ruins created a journey for me and brought me to an era that I never even knew about.

To my understanding, this is where one of the darkest parts of Irish history is hidden. It is often referred to as "The Great Famine." I understand this was actually a starvation of the Irish by absentee British land agents who charged outrageous amounts of money for land but also took food raised by locals and gave it to their lords for their own survival. Regardless of the potato blight that occurred, other crops were available that the Irish could use, including food from livestock such as goats milk.

A closer view of the ruins left behind when those who fled this area and sought new lands during the Irish "Famine" as it has been recorded in history, abandoned their homes.

I came to learn that this is where the term boycott was developed. Captain Charles Boycott, who was an estate agent for an absentee British land agent, had his "tenants" turn against him by refusing to pay monies or do any work. As such, they boycotted they land.

The graveyard that lies near the entrance to the Deserted Village.

The journey that day was both magical and haunting. My Aunt Josephine and Uncle Thomas, both whom have since left this world, brought us to Achill to explore the picturesque landscape that this part of Ireland held in beauty and in secret. Thousands of those from this area left in what were known as coffin ships and set sail for new lands. Many did not make it.

On that awe-inspiring day in August of 1998 and before descending upon the village, we found a gravesite at the base of the path and took the time to pay our respects to the deceased that are interned there. We looked at their gravestones and learned about a part of Irish history.

From here my spiritual journey to learn about the events that occurred during the 1840s began. This was not from just any storyteller or tour guide, but from the people themselves of that era. The visions they shared with me were astonishing and provided a greater understanding of a life that had been.

## The Enchantment of Achill

The journey began on a long winding road,
This day of adventure was about to unfold.
The car, it did stop at the foot of the hill,
My heart, it beat fast; I could hardly sit still.

I stood in amazement at the Celtic gravesite,
Which watched over our ancestors by day and by night.
And now their village I would carefully explore,
But how was I to know I would discover so much more?

I ascended the slope, my eyes they sat wide,
With the beauty around me I was filled with such pride.
But all of a sudden things they would change,
Was I going mad, or could I be strange?

My ears, they perked up at the wonderful sound,
Of Irish war pipes, but they were nowhere to be found.
I scanned the horizon; I looked left and right,
I looked all around, but still no one was in sight.

I turned to my aunt and asked her the same,
"Can you hear the war pipes that now roam in my brain?"
"I hear them indeed," was her reply to me,
"Do not be afraid; let your spirit roam free."

I let myself relax and began to feel at peace,
The pipes of great sadness then seemed to cease.
I cleared up my mind and focused my gaze,
The sheep were not bothered; they continued to graze.

I stood at the village, which was once full of life,
Until Captain Boycott came, so bitter with strife.
He worked those poor people and left them in vain,
"You'll work in the sunlight; you'll work in the rain."

My legs walked easily into each of the homes,
My hands traced freely, touching each of the stones.
I stood in these ruins with such delicate care,
My ancestors of the past watched over my stare.

The others, they left and descended the hill,
My spirit was strong, and so was my will.
I put down my camera and closed my eyes,
And boy was I in for a major surprise.

I brought up my left hand to cover my face,
And felt those good souls lift me to their place.
Cast back to their day when their lives were so free,
They were such a proud people; this was easy to see.

I heard words of excitement escape from my throat,
I watched in awe, and this I do quote.
"Making food, harvesting land, with not one penny to pay,
Tending to sheep, milking goats, we will survive another day."

I felt a great rush sweep right though my soul,
My spirit quickly ignited, I totally felt whole.
By these ancestors of ours who worked hard on the land,
Brought me to their era, and amongst them I did stand.

When the time, it did come, for me to move down,
Back to the Celtic gravesites, I thought I might frown.
But when I reflected on my experience back a short mile,
I thanked my ancestors for making me smile.

They opened my soul and my spirit so deep,
They strengthened my flame, which was so weak.
They brought me back without any wrath,
So that I might complete my journey and my path.

In this life in which I have been placed,
I carry the torch, I carry the faith.
For those who are down and feel right out,
I share all my energies to remove all their doubt.

So if with this poem you may chance to read,
Plant the next positive energy of life-giving seed.
Before you give up and close the door,
Think of my ancestors and the cross that they bore.

# In The Name of Religion

OFTENTIMES I HAVE heard people say that the Irish are the salt of the earth and that they are the most easygoing and wonderful people, always quick for a bit of craic and to lift a pint, who are very helpful when it comes to giving directions and hospitality to lost tourists.

With that being said, we were just one of thousands of families exposed to the political and religious persecutions. As a result, we immigrated so we could live a peaceful existence. I wonder if we will ever live in peace—not just in Northern Ireland, but the world over. Will humans ever understand that the wars we wage against each other should be targeted against HIV, leukemia, poverty, cancer, tuberculosis, corruption, and corporate greed?

I am not sure that I could truly capture the years of hatred that existed and that over 3,700 lives were lost during "The Troubles," with thousands of others impacted. Although things have settled down quite a bit, there remain constant flare-ups. The only way to gain an understanding or appreciation of our lives is to decide from one's own views and opinions.

Condemned labels were used to describe my siblings and me. We were constantly chased, stopped, questioned, and beaten time and time again for growing up in the land of our ancestors, and were only able to truly appreciate our heritage and identities upon leaving for new land.

In trying to best protect her children, my mum christened us with English names so those who targeted Catholics would not identify us. We were not granted the beautiful Celtic names we so often hear nowadays, names that my own two children have been given. Our very identities and heritage were stripped from us because we were Irish. Those who targeted us had other names in mind, such as "Fenian" and "Taige." We were also targeted because of our school uniforms and the church we attended. Even though we left in 1985, we have yet to leave those scars from our childhoods behind.

I recall in the late seventies and early eighties my mum panicking because my older siblings Karen and Joe, who attended grammar school in Belfast, did not make it home. Incidents like this happened quite frequently. The reason for this is that many job opportunities were awarded to the Protestant majority, while Catholics were left to fend for themselves. As such, Catholic school children were often left standing in the pouring rain as bus drivers, recognizing them due to their school uniforms, would drive on by.

One of the worst incidents that occurred was on May 5, 1981, when after sixty-six days of refusing food and water, the first hunger striker died. I remember my mum screaming at the top of her lungs and scrambling to get her car into Belfast. Riots had broken out, and two of her children were again left stranded by bus drivers. Getting to my sister and brother was an arduous task, as barricades and checkpoints had been erected by our police force, the Royal Ulster Constabulary. Again, this force was made up of a 95 percent majority of people from one religion. To this day, I have yet to understand how religion makes one person better than another.

Another incident occurred when Karen—although not wearing her school uniform on this particular day—was identified by a group of school-aged girls, who pointed her out as being a "Fenian." The school-aged boys that were with them chased my sister for three miles, knives in hand and threatening to cut her to shreds. This is no different from the day a group of individuals dragged her to a place called Nellie's dam and tried to drown her in the stream that flowed near our house. The water in the dam was deep – her attempted drowning in the name of religion.

There have been incidents of many Irish families being forcefully evicted from their homes due to letter bombs being pushed through their front doors. Other incidents involve Molotov cocktails, also known as petrol bombs being smashed through the living room windows of peoples' houses. Attempts such as these have been successfully utilized in burning Catholics out of their homes and the districts in which they lived.

Our school gym was used to conduct Sunday Mass, with an altar erected on the stage. However, in 1979 and while in attendance at the youth club, a group of individuals from one of the most bitter of areas in Belfast came to the club, began damaging property, and before leaving took great pleasure in urinating all over the altar. What could possess anyone to become so hateful of another individual because of his or her religious belief?

Sadly though, and long after us leaving Northern Ireland, this hatred continued. In September 2001, a young Protestant man was shot dead after he was mistakenly identified as being a Catholic. Three months prior, a Catholic church we attended as kids was burnt to the ground. Individuals from differing religions have also been beaten or killed due to dating a person of the opposite religion. Distraught children attending Holy Cross Primary School were attacked with blast bombs and feces-filled balloons and had to be escorted through police barricades to get to school. The appalling images are on YouTube. But why does this happen? Incidents such as these are completely senseless.

I am ashamed at how this exposes our world today. Humans full of hate, anger, and bitterness against other humans due to their background: race, religion, culture, skin colour, language, and sexual orientation – the list is endless. This needs to stop immediately. We need to begin breaking down the cultural, socio-economic, structural, and political barriers that divide us. Although we are all individual in our own right, we need to respect others for being different from us. We need to collectively embrace humanity – one day at a time and not in the name of religion.

# Shenanigans of the Scattered Youth

T HERE HAVE BEEN so many other memories that have come to my mind that I look back at with extremely fond appreciation. These are part of my carefree days growing up amongst the sectarian hatred that creeped into my neighbourhood. I hold those memories near and dear to my heart and mind, and I will not allow someone else's bitter views to take them from me due to their own self-destructive behaviour.

### Belfast Telegraph

When I was about thirteen years of age, I decided to take a job out of the Woodford shops to deliver the *Belfast Telegraph* evening edition. This arrived fresh off the presses each day around half-four. I had a route consisting of twenty-two papers to be delivered to the Woodford, Fairview, Glenkyle, and Christine districts. These were quite similar to my own middle-class neighbourhood, made up of people from both sides of the religious divide.

We weren't paid much, but in our day it was as if we had a fortune on our hands and could buy whatever sweets we wanted at the end of the week when we collected our rations. The shops consisted of a newsagent, a post office, a chemist, a greengrocer, as well as a hair salon on the upper floor of the building that required people to climb several steps to reach.

One of my mates who lived about four doors from the shops would take the lead and count out to each of us how many papers we needed for our deliveries when the storekeeper was busy looking after other customers. I'd take the papers, my hands covered in fresh black ink, and load up my bag, which eventually changed from cloth to a thick vinyl exterior to keep the rain off, since it bucketed that much and the papers got drenched while I made my rounds.

I often thought how awfully nice it was of the *Telegraph* to take this approach to ensure their papers would safely get into the hands of their readership, but this didn't save them from me. There were countless days I would use the papers to protect myself from getting half-drowned due to the torrential downpours we faced so often.

I always had an interest in being a drummer, and so as I walked along the streets to where I was supposed to make my deliveries, I'd take two of the neatly pressed and folded papers out of my bag, roll them tightly into thick drumsticks, and start smacking them against the exterior of the bag while marching to my own beat. The papers didn't take kindly to this, and the day's headlines would literally have the shite knocked out of them before they made it to the letterbox of each residence along my route.

As soon as I made the delivery, out would come another paper, and I would make another drumstick. I never did ask if the subscribers appreciated my efforts to teach myself to play the drums with that evening's headlines.

I remember one house along my route in Woodford that had a small fluffy dog. It was the most vicious wee bugger you can find, and would eat the face off you if given the chance. It would sit and wait for me to deliver the paper, and if it fell from the letterbox all the way inside the front door, the dog would shred the paper into pieces and leave it in a state that would only be good for starting a fire.

The owners of the house had two children: a daughter who was younger than me, and a son who was older than I but was a miserable auld bastard. He would pick on me when our paths crossed. Although I was careful to ensure the newspaper did not fall to the ground once I placed it in their letterbox, his attitude and prior engagement of me on the streets determined if I would give the paper an extra push to mess up his anticipation of the day's headlines with the help of their dog.

## Kamikaze Catwalks

Due to the building of other estates around our once peaceful neighbourhood, we very soon found ourselves facing the same rubbish and began to get repeatedly targeted by individuals who were not a part of our friendship circles. For whatever reason, they felt they had the right to bring their views of hatred into our area, even though we were from a mixed community and got along very well. This may have also been in part to our choice of music, as there were different genres that went out of their way to beat the living daylights out of one another, depending on whether you identified as being a mod, skinhead, teddy, punk, or into heavy metal.

In order to get ourselves out of sticky situations—as well as to have a bit of fun—Joe and his mates, who were a part of the Woodford Heavies, along with Denis and I would teach ourselves how to navigate the streets by barely stepping foot on them. Joe would show me how to leave the back garden of our own house and cross in and out of approximately fifteen houses that made up our street as well as the street behind us. We did this by climbing fences, sneaking behind fir trees that lined the bottom of gardens, and hiding behind sheds.

We'd call this "going for a catwalk," although we did not stop there, and would continue our efforts into neighbouring streets so as to learn what routes were safe and what were not.

We would run up to the chain link fences that surrounded a neighbouring school—built to help serve the newly created district—and would learn how to jump while diving over it into a forward roll once on the other side. Our belief was that this would help us get quite a few strides on our pursuers once we managed to get back into an upright stance after clearing the fence. Being quite a bit smaller than Joe and Denis, I found myself getting hung up on the top of the fence at times, and would be left with serious abdominal bruising. I would never learn my lesson.

One night a large group of us were out messing about in the streets and it was around half-two in the morning. We were hanging around the Woodford shops, only to look down towards the bottom of the Woodford Road and see a paddy wagon coming straight for us. We were not used to seeing these vehicles in our neighbourhood. They were very ominous, almost the same colour schemes as associated with "The Daleks," which put just as much fear into us from the British television show *Doctor Who*.

We bolted in separate directions, as we did not want to get picked up by the peelers. Joe and I took off and dove over a wall at the top of Woodford Drive that had a heavy, full growth of fir trees behind it, but it was about a three-foot drop to the garden below. We pushed ourselves up against the wall, and Joe whispered to me to not breathe or move.

The trees provided us with excellent cover, as only a moment later we heard heavy boots walk above us, one of the men saying, "I'm sure some of them went this way." We must have lay there for a good twenty minutes, holding our

The Woodford Shops. On either side of the building are the steps up to the businesses on the second level. We would play penny poker at the top of the steps (out of sight), or use these as part of our playground and practice area to hone our escape skills.

collective breaths while waiting for one of our other mates to give everyone else the signal that the coast was clear.

Another tactic was to go to the Woodford shops and scale a number of steps to the business located on the second floor of the building. We'd teach each other how to climb the wall and grab onto the pipe that stuck out of the wall beneath our feet on the other side. We'd lower ourselves down to the pipe and hang from it with our arms outstretched above our heads before dropping to the surface below again.

We would practice this so often that it almost became second nature, as well as perhaps a sideshow for those who didn't believe we could pull such a feat off without breaking our necks in the process. I would hazard a guess and say this was at least a twenty to twenty-five foot drop, but we were willing to take extreme measures to ensure we could get out of whatever situation we found ourselves in.

### Man in the Coveralls

You'd think we'd have learned our lessons after run-ins like these, but there was one night we truly believed we'd developed our best plans ever, which had been carefully calculated earlier that day.

Once again Joe and I had planned to go around to Denis's house and call on him in the middle of the night. We decided we were going to walk around the streets of Knockview and Woodford, across the SADOW field, and into the forest along the Doagh Road. There really wasn't much else about for us to do except try our hand at spinning trick yoyos when they came out, adding graffiti to the walls at the shops, riding our bikes, or playing Stick the Knife.

On this particular night, Denis had snuck out of his house to meet up with Joe and myself at a pre-arranged location. We weren't doing anyone harm but simply walking around our neighbourhood talking about AC/DC, Black Sabbath, and other bands we listened to. It was also to have the freedom of being out from under our parents' set times and rules for when they thought we should be in our beds. We were rebels without a cause and often without a clue.

But after spending about two-and-a-half hours out on the streets, and while walking Denis back to his house along Knockview Avenue, we saw a shadowy, cloak-like figure coming towards us from much further down the road. No, it wasn't Lord Voldemort from the Harry Potter books as written by one of my most favourite and inspirational authors, J.K. Rowling, but as there was nothing out of the ordinary about this individual, we decided to lower our voices to keep our conversations to ourselves and to try and not let on that we should not have been out on the streets at that hour.

Knockview Avenue, with the Doagh Road forest and Knockagh Monument in the distance. We had plenty of places to hide and practice our kamikaze catwalks.

We could see from the street lamps that the man had an anorak on over a pair of work jeans that were well-worn, and the faux-fur lined hood of his anorak was fully zipped up. There was no telltale sign in advance for us to know who this person was until he stopped right in front of us, unzipped his hood, lowered it, and said those fateful words…

"What are you doing out here?"

We were busted. Before Joe or I could respond, Denis said that we had come to get him. His dad looked between the three of us, and I'm sure the look on our faces went pale as if we had seen a ghost. We were told to go home as my mate did the same and walked in the opposite direction away from us with his father, who stood like a giant over us. He put us in Coventry – meaning we weren't allowed to speak to one another for at least a week.

After we were allowed to speak, what we had found out was that our carefully crafted plan *had* gone exactly as we had discussed earlier that day. We'd followed our own instructions to a perfect execution.

Denis had tucked a pillow into his bed along with some clothes to make it look like he was sleeping. However, when his dad entered the room after getting home from work that night, Denis's younger brother John blurted out that we had gone out together, throwing our carefully developed plans out the window. We didn't stand a chance. Perhaps if we had gotten John a Mars Bar and a bag of Tayto Cheese and Onion crisps and a tin of coke we could have bought his silence. Or, we should have given him a bag of Basset's Jelly Babies to glue his mouth shut.

We may also have been able to exercise our stealth-like cat-walking abilities, simply disappearing into one of the back gardens and getting Denis home without ever being caught on the streets. If only his dad had been wearing what we normally associated him with… coveralls.

Denis's father was known for wearing coveralls from the crack of dawn to the dusk of night, or so it seemed. He was a brilliant, hardworking, and dedicated man to his family, and he had become like a second father to me over the years while my own dad was at sea. However, anytime any of us would see him working in his garage, on his car, or out in the garden, we wondered if these coveralls were surgically attached to him, because they never seemed to leave his body. They were a part of his identity, like a second skin of sorts. We thought he perhaps used these as his pajamas, and if that had indeed been the case during the early hours of that fateful morning, we would have spotted him a mile away, making like magicians and disappearing into the night while thwarting the Man in the Coveralls.

I must give him credit, for when I was home in 2010, and if for only a few hours, he did indeed manage to shed this outer skin for a suit when his beautiful daughter Rosie was married. I almost didn't recognize him all dressed up with someplace to go.

### Escape from Carrick Castle

There was one situation we found ourselves in where the catwalk technique would come to our rescue. In 1984, along with Joe, a bunch of our mates and I decided to go down to the marina that sits beside Carrickfergus Castle, which is a Norman stronghold built in 1177 and sits on the northern shores of Belfast Lough. When we were children attending primary school, we used to take trips to visit the castle and learn about this impressive structure and its history. These days it is a tourist attraction, and there is also a famous song about Carrickfergus.

A bunch of us got our fishing rods out and dug up worms from among the rose bushes in the back garden. We made our way on our bicycles out of our neighbourhoods of Knockview and Woodford, onto the Old Carrick Road, and down Troopers Lane to the Belfast Road, where we would make the final leg of our trek to the castle itself. For a group of teens, this six-and-a-half mile trek was by no means going to be an easy feat.

While we were all down by the marina catching mostly crabs or slimy eels, which are considered an export delicacy from the loughs in and around Northern Ireland, Joe asked if I wanted to head into the castle as he had a few pounds on him and could get the two of us in.

We left our fishing rods with our mates and cycled up the ramp of the castle and under the portcullis before parking our bikes by the front entrance. Joe paid our way, and we went to explore the historic walls of this keep without the watchful eyes of any teachers.

After taking in all the attractions, at one point we somehow ended up in one of the lower dungeon areas, which were off-limits. From here we were able to reach out and speak to our mates through the grates that barred the narrow slots that acted as windows. Two of them came up to see what we were doing, so we asked if they would like to come in to join us. As they didn't have tickets, we decided to give them ours, and if asked at the gate, they would say they had bought them earlier that day and wanted to come in for another look around. We also said, "Whatever you do, DON'T mention our names or that you got these from us."

Great planning, but definitely not great execution. When our two mates got to the gate, something went horribly wrong.

Joe and I were mucking about the castle checking out the various coats of arms, knights' chainmail and armour used so many centuries before. We were about to make our way down to the lower level to meet up with our mates, but we could hear a set of high heels loudly clicking across the floor along with two authoritative voices announcing that they were looking for us. Yet again, we'd been busted.

The plan that seemed bulletproof must have been filled with holes. Our fears were that our two mates had been interrogated, threatened with a tar and feathering, or tortured and impaled within the confines of an iron maiden if they did not give us up. Obviously they had, as the staff knew our names and had descriptions of what we were wearing that day.

At the time, and if the music for *Mission Impossible* had been available, it would have been a fitting piece for this exact moment. We'd spent many hours in the evenings under the cloak of darkness practicing our cat-walking techniques, jumping down from the sides of walls to plan our escapes as well as other tactics we could use if we ever needed to utilize a quick getaway. There was no time like the present to put these plans and efforts into full action.

As we were wearing our soft-soled guddies, we had a bit of an advantage over the staff, since they could not detect us scurrying across the floors of the castle. We bolted in one direction to take an extremely worn stone staircase back down to the lower level, as we had only just come up this way in an attempt to escape without being spotted. However, as soon as we hit the top step and began our descent, we could hear the voices of staff. "They might have come up this way." They began their ascent towards us. Our exit was blocked, and so we had to turn back.

Joe took me on a full sprint from within this mighty structure to the outside walls, where archers would have stood many centuries before to protect the castle from encroaching ships. This was an upper wall. The problem was we had no way down except to jump into the grassy courtyard below. It was not an immediate option for either of us.

Joe wasted no time. While keeping his head low, he instructed me to do the same as we snuck along the wall and down to where our getaway Raleigh Choppers were waiting for us in the exact same spot we'd left them. Call it a premonition, but on this day we did not lock our bikes up. This would aid in our terrifying escape from the staff in full pursuit of us.

My brother lowered himself to his knees and hung unto the edge of the wall before sliding his legs over the edge and dropped to the lawn area below. I hesitated for a moment only to be prompted by him. "C'mon. Hurry up, will ye?" I immediately took the same leap of faith below with a dead thud. The fall winded me, but with the adrenaline surge pumping through my body, I didn't have time to think about it. We had to get away as if there was no tomorrow.

There must have been smoke billowing from the chains on our bikes and tyres as we pedaled our arses down the ramp as fast and as furiously as our legs would allow us. We arrived back at the safety of the marina, where our mates now stood with stunned looks on their faces. Obviously we lived to tell the tale and did not become permanent fixtures within the dungeon walls themselves. I never went back until 2010, hoping that twenty-six years would have at least erased the memory of our escape from Carrick Castle from their black books.

### Car on the Beak

On a particular winter's day in 1982, a bunch of my mates along with Joe and I were mucking about at the top of our street of Knockview Park and along Knockview Road, which had a steep incline to it. At the bottom of this street was a yellow bin with the letters D.O.E. stamped on it. Within this was a mixture of salt, sand, and grit to help people gain traction during our winter months, as our streets were not sanded or ploughed.

Every time we noticed a vehicle turning from the Doagh Road onto our playground we'd shout, "Car on the beak!" to warn each other before moving off to the footpaths and watching the car struggle to get traction. This wasn't helped by our efforts to shine the surface by sliding down the road on our honkers. The tyres would spin, and the vehicle would move

The steep incline associated to Knockview Road, with Knockview Avenue to the left and the top of my street on the right. The Doagh Road forest stands at the bottom of the road, and was part of our playground.

forward ever so slowly before the driver realized he or she would need to take a bit of a run at the steep incline of Knockview Road, subsequently backing up.

After several attempts without much success, we'd offer the driver a push, since there were enough of us around to help. Before the driver could thank us for being perfect angels, we had our own schemes already planned out as to how this would benefit us.

We informed the driver that Knockview Avenue was just off to the right, and would provide them with a greater chance to get traction. Once they made it partially up Knockview Road, they should take the opportunity as aided by our efforts to get onto this street and on their way.

We would get in behind the vehicle and push, although we also purposely failed to inform the driver that this street was also extremely slick, since we'd had a beak with every other car that faced the same quandary as they were at that moment.

In one instance, a gentleman driving a Ford Cortina was having the same predicament. While pushing, heaving, and struggling with every ounce of determination, one of us shouted for him to turn onto Knockview Avenue. Following our instruction and celebrating that our joint efforts had paid off, we immediately grabbed a hold of his back bumper while sliding along the street.

We maybe went the length of approximately three houses when suddenly the bumper dislodged from the car and completely broke free. We were left stunned, crouched down, our arses barely above the surface of the snow and ice-packed road with a piece of this man's car gripped firmly in our collective hands.

In an instant we came to the realization of what just happened, and for whatever reason we stood up, raised the long piece of metal above our heads, and began chasing after the car, all the while shouting, "Hey mister! Come back. You forgot your bumper!

Mister, come back, will ye." But his brake lights never came on. The man wouldn't slow down. In all honesty and looking back on that day, I certainly don't blame him either as if it had of been me looking in my rear view mirror at a bunch of wee lads chasing me with a bumper in their hands, I would have drove on myself.

Knockview Avenue was quite slick from our efforts to have a beak with every other car. We placed the man's bumper just past the lamppost in the distance on the left.

During this time there was a poster campaign titled "Keep Newtownabbey Tidy." As there was nothing more we could do since the man had driven on, we neatly left his bumper on the side of the footpath in case he decided to come back for it later and after he'd come to the realization that our angelic efforts to assist him had other outcomes.

A S MUCH AS people love Irish accents and find them to be an attractive quality, I personally believe they are a curse. I end up constantly having to explain myself.

While in conversation and without realization, I often end up saying, "Aye… Aye… Aye..." as the discussion unfolds.

Suddenly the person who is speaking to me would stop and say, "Eye. What's wrong with your eyes? You keep talking about them. Are they alright?"

To which I would respond, "Ack, it's not me eyes, it's me ayes, and they're fine."

The Irish also have a habit of responding with, "Ack aye. Ack right. Ack sure I know what you mean" throughout the entire conversation. What I have yet to figure out though is how they know exactly what it is that I mean when this could very well be the first time they've heard me tell them the story. My mum used to tell my siblings and me she had eyes on the back of her head and knew everything that we were up to. The Irish must also have powers of telepathy.

I've heard there is a common expression used openly in Dublin when shopping at the greengrocers. While selecting various produce for texture and quality, the shopkeeper will say without a second thought, "Don't be touching all my fruits and vegetables, you auld huer ye." This is not a derogative expression. It is simply a part of our language and is interwoven into our culture. But the sayings do not end there.

The kindness of the Irish is very much unmatched anywhere in the world. Often when I've gone home to visit relatives or friends, they'll say, "Greg. Here's a wee drop in your hawn," meaning I cannot leave their company without first taking a cup of tea and a biscuit such as a chocolate covered McVitties digestive, a few jaffa cakes, or even some Cadbury's fingers. If ever I refuse, they'll say, "Ack, c'mon now, Greg, you can't expect to come round and not have a wee cuppa. Ack, go on, you'll have just a wee cup won'tcha? How about a half-cup? Aye, you'll take a half-cup. Lovely. I'll go ahead and put the kettle on."

After accepting their kind offer and while untwisting my arm, what they may not realize is that my bladder is floating from all the tea I had to drink at everyone else's house. My belly is bloated and my teeth are near rotted from all the chocolate biscuits I had to consume, so as to not cause serious offense by rejecting their warm hospitality. Needless to say, it could also be seen as forgiveness when they come off with one of their most brutally honest of statements: "Greg, you're looking well these days. You've put on a bit of weight."

The Irish are quick to have a celebration for just about anything, including death. Our approach to this can be awkward, as we are known to love "the drink." I've heard horror stories of people buying the morning paper and while sitting over breakfast, will scour the obituaries to plan out their day. They then go to

Lifting a half pint to celebrate St. Patrick's Day 2011 in Newcastle, County Down. Although legend says St. Patrick chased all of the snakes out of Ireland, my take on this is that they became politicians and formed government!

the local church to pick up a mass card, and ask the priest to offer up a prayer for the soul of the deceased.

After making their way around to where the wake is being held, they ask, "Is this where the dead man lives?" Once confirmed, they offer sincerest condolences, and give a few words of how the deceased would be sorely missed, while making up a load of complete and utter shite as to how they knew that person. They would then proceed with their original intent to have a few pints, a couple of sandwiches, and a jaffa cake or two at the expense of the grieving relatives.

The Irish use a lot of banter, slagging, and humour when speaking to someone from our family or to our friends, and is usually accompanied by a ton of swear words. We believe this adds colour to our language, although this is not meant to be slanderous or malicious in its intent or approach. It's just how we engage each other.

Being an ex-pat, I've hung onto sayings that are called "Belfastisms" which make up a part of my regular vocabulary. These can get me into trouble even though they are considered normal back home.

And so while home for a funeral in 2011, I decided to drive over to Country Fermanagh. As I was driving along, I saw a garage up ahead that had a sign on the outside showing an ice cream cone, with a Cadbury's flake in it. We would call these a "ninety nine."

Since this used to be one of my most favourite treats as a child, I pulled in to the garage to get one. I walked up to the counter, where two young ladies were standing. I took a few coins out from my pocket and after being acknowledged by the clerk, simply said, "Hiya. Can you give us a poke?"

The girl who was standing directly in front of me went pale white, as if she had seen a ghost. Her eyes were as wide as saucers. In an exasperated voice, she exclaimed, "Can I give you a what?" The other girl standing to her left went into a complete fit of laughter at my request and what she thought was an indecent proposal.

I repeated the same statement. "Can you give us a poke?"

By this time, her face had gone to fifty shades of embarrassed. The other girl continued to howl with laughter.

Seeing that this conversation was not going the way I had originally intended, I turned to the pensioner standing beside me and asked, "Am I in Norn Iron? Do you know what I'm after?"

"Aye," replied the wee woman. "You're wanting an ice cream. We called them pokes in my day too. We also used to buy a poke of chips." I had never heard them called that before and only associated a poke with an ice cream.

A picture of an ice cream cone with a double flake in it along with raspberry sauce on top is also known as a "poke."

Understanding what I was now after, the wee girl behind the counter steadied her hand, pulled the cone for me, stuck the flake into the top, and added a few strands of raspberry sauce. I must admit that I am a little more careful now when asking for a cone.

Over the years and on the several occasions that I've gone home, more than a few close friends of mine including Jeff, Heath, and Krista, who live here in Canada and have known me for well over twenty-five years, have and still say that they only understand about forty percent of what I say upon my arrival back from Belfast. Oftentimes, I'll be chatting with people only to see their heads nodding up and down and smiling back at me. I call this the "classic Canadian look." For whatever reason, they believe they're being polite although they haven't a clue what I'm talking about.

I've learned to watch for that body language and for that very reason will say, "Do you see this motion of me nodding my head up and down? That means yes in Ireland. Now, do you see me moving my head left and right? Well, that means no in Ireland. It's universal and works just as well back home as it does here, so if you don't understand me, just shake your head no."

Unfortunately, this does not apply to every segment of the population. In my working years as a cable technician, it was about half-eight during a snowy winter's night. I had to attend a senior's complex to do a service call. The complaint listed on the work order was that the subscriber was not happy at having French on her television. When I arrived at her door, I could see she was visibly upset.

Her first words to me were that she did not speak French, she did not like the French, and she did not want French on her TV set and wanted it off immediately. As this is carried through the cable stream, the most I could do was to reprogram her television so that when she changed the stations, it would skip the channels in question.

This was not good enough for her. She became extremely angry. I tried to reason with her, saying that Canada is a bilingual country and I wish they carried a Gaelic channel so I could perhaps identify with my lost language. My efforts were unfortunately not good enough for her.

After forty-five minutes of explaining how the system works, she demanded a discount on her basic cable package. I informed her that this was beyond my control and likely would not occur, as the cost is shared among all subscribers. She would need to speak to a supervisor in the hopes of getting some sort of refund, if at all possible.

As I had other service calls waiting, I said I needed to go but would give her the phone number to the office and offered to let them know that I had tried to resolve her complaint.

Standing with a pen and paper in her hand and in a stern, determined, and demanding voice, she said, "Give me the number to the cable company."

I blurted out the seven digits she needed: "Seven-eighty… eighty-eight… eighty-eight…"

The lady's eyes widened, her face flushed, and as she looked at me with furrowed eyebrows, she exclaimed, "Excuse me, son? I don't appreciate you calling me names!"

I almost fell over at her comment. "Pardon me, ma'am?"

She responded, "I don't appreciate you calling me names!"

I looked at her with a shocked and aghast expression on my face and said, "I'm sorry, ma'am, but I didn't call you any names whatsoever. What names do you think I called you?"

She said, "You called me an idiot and you called me it twice!"

My brain was scrambling at this point because for the life of me I had no idea how she had even come to that conclusion. But it has since been pointed out that those of us from Norn Iron don't pronounce our vowels. Thankfully for me, the lady had her daughter there, a schoolteacher who calmed her mum down and explained I was from another country and spoke differently, even though I was indeed giving her the correct phone number.

Speaking of seniors, my dad recently came by my house and asked if my children Caitlin, Ciarán, and I would like to go out for a meal. I've been told that my dad has a very strong brogue and when he and I speak, my *own* accent becomes just as thick as it was the day I left.

In always trying to be a comedian, my dad thought he would have a bit of a wind at our server by saying, "I'm a senior, so that means I get half-price on my meal, right?" Knowing the stunts he constantly tries to pull when the two of us are out together and that his comments are always the same, I turned to the server and said, "Here, don't you be listening to him, mate. That's my dad. He's half senile."

Upon hearing this, my father erupted: "Whad'ya mean your dad? I'm yer da!" He missed my term of endearment.

My kids were left wondering if an all-out war was about to occur. They couldn't help but laugh at the craic I was coming off with about their granda without any swearing.

The slaggin' did not stop there, continuing all throughout supper and into the parking lot where I started into him about how he had parked his car. I said, "Would you look at the state of that parking job, da? You're as crooked as a dog's back leg." He tried to shield the attention away from himself towards his granddaughter, without success.

We went our separate ways. Upon arriving home, I decided to log onto the Belfast Child Facebook page to post an update. While the "likes" came in, I responded to Teresa, whom I have had the pleasure of chatting back and forth with about our language of the days gone by and the way we speak. I wrote, "I went back to look at some of our conversations tonight, as I wanted to write about a wee millie who I was speaking with and the craic we shared."

Originally, a wee millie was a name given to girls who came from low to middle-class neighbourhoods in and around Belfast, and who used to work at the old spinning mills. However, although this term has evolved over the years throughout the UK it is less than flattering in its meaning but meant as a bit of craic.

Teresa responded, "Am I that wee millie you refer to, ya wee ballix! I'll shove my brush pole so far up your hole, I'll leave you looking like a candy apple!"

She would later write to me to say that she was "in a wrinkle" from our online exchange. My response was that there are some great anti-aging products, which are quite effective in helping to prevent wrinkling. A different culture with a very different perspective of language! To be able to laugh at one's self is to be able to laugh at the world around us.

This wee poem is for my beautiful and amazing First Nations friend, Jade Harper, who has a desire to head overseas and take the opportunity to tour around the North of Ireland and see all it has to offer, including a bit of craic and an Ulster fry. Hopefully once you're there, a translator will help you understand half of what the people are saying. Perhaps this "Irish Anishinabe" can take on the task and get a free trip out of it? If not, simply nod your head up and down and smile, Jade. It works for some people over here in Canada. Well, about forty percent of the time.

## Belfast Craic

A toast with a pint of Guinness,
Is how we raise a jar.
And if we talk about the boot,
We mean the trunk of a car.

If we say he's blootered,
What we're saying is he's drunk.
To say that something's boggin',
We're saying that it stunk.

If you're told to shut yer gub,
It's better not to talk.
And if we tell you to take a hike,
It's not a mountain walk.

If you're told to go and shite,
That does not mean the bathroom calls.
But if we ask where to find a bog,
We need the toilet stalls.

If you're asked "What's the craic?"
Have you any news to tell?
If you've a face like a busted sausage,
It means you're as ugly as hell.

If told you're a buck eejit,
We mean you're a nutcase.
If your bake looks like a Lurgan spade,
You're looking really long in the face.

When told something's dead on,
It must be really good.
When told to take yourself off by the hand,
You've put me in a bad mood.

When told to put the fire on,
It means a shovel of coal.
If you don't do what you're told,
You'll get my toe up your hole.

MUSIC HAS ALWAYS been a huge part of my life, from when my brother introduced me to "I love Rock 'n' Roll" by Joan Jett and the Blackhearts, to my first taste of AC/DC through a 45" single he had called "Let There Be Rock." With that said, many of us have childhood idols that come in various forms: action figures, Hollywood heroes, famous writers, or musicians. Such musicians are the reason that this composition came together, and it is based on a trio of legendary brothers from Northern Ireland who rocked the world

Tommy, Pat, and John McManus, who made up Irish rock band Mama's Boys. Here, I met my childhood idols during the Power and Passion World Tour concert held in Winnipeg, on September 22, 1985.

Molly, the original vocalist for the band before the rise of Pulse, and sister of Pat, John, and Tommy. This photo was taken in 2008 after a private two-day concert featuring Pat, joined onstage by Bernie Marsden of Whitesnake.

not only with their brilliant and influential music, but their tremendous interaction with and dedication to their fans.

Pat "The Professor," John, and Tommy McManus grew up near the small village of Derrylin, County Fermanagh, Northern Ireland. They started off their young musical careers playing traditional Irish music. Pat won several medals and awards for his brilliance on the fiddle and became the All Irish Champion at age fourteen. John was a champion tin whistle player and was extremely skilled on the Irish Uilleann bagpipe. Tommy kept a steady beat on the Irish drum: the Bodhrán.

They formed a band called Pulse but before had put together a musical foursome with their sister on vocals. Molly, if you chance a read of this, I'm hoping you've kept some of the bootlegs from your early days, as I'd like a copy with an autograph.

The boys took a great interest in rock 'n' roll, with bands such as Budgie, Rush, and Black Sabbath, but Thin Lizzy and Horslips were also among their favourites. Their love for rock music started to creep into their lives even more. From this, their dear father, John Sr., who was also a champion fiddle player, would ask Pat to slow down as he tore up the frets on the family's guitar. One day though, he surprised the family when he brought a bass guitar home and

**Mama's Boys: Tommy, Pat, and John.**

eventually a drum kit. Shortly thereafter, the development of songwriting for Pulse began taking shape.

The name of the band changed after a Radio Luxembourg DJ jokingly called them mama's boys due to their young age. After all, Tommy was only thirteen-years-old in 1979 when they began touring with Irish rock legends – Horslips. The name stuck.

My appreciation for the band began back in 1984. A friend from school who was a headbanger was crazy about the rock band KISS. He told me about Mama's Boys and prompted me to pick up their music. With monies made from delivering the *Belfast Telegraph,* I would catch a bus down to the city centre and go into the local record shops to buy their albums.

The first record I ever bought was their self-titled disk, which became an instant hit on my brother's record player. I would take every opportunity when he was out to play this album, and while shamelessly headbanging to the beat, I'd sing along to whatever lyrics I could pull off and remember. I was definitely no match to John's voice, but would do my best to impersonate his look and style, quite often with failure.

**May 23, 1988 with Guns N' Roses drummer, Steven Adler, in support of their *Appetite For Destruction* album. They opened for Iron Maiden.**

**Bruce Dickinson, vocalist for Iron Maiden, during their *7th Tour of a 7th Tour.***

One Saturday, I caught the bus into Belfast and made yet another purchase. Gleaming in my hand shortly thereafter was their latest release called *Power and Passion*, which also happened to come with a twelve-inch picture disc and featured the song "One Last Chance." On the reserve side was an interview featuring Pat, John, and Tommy as recorded in Battery studios in London. A fellow I knew from school saw me walking along Royal Avenue and asked what I had bought. I proudly displayed my still newly wrapped purchase, much to his displeasure. He did not follow my interests in music, but I didn't really care what he thought, as I was much more interested in getting back to my house to play this latest offering from my favourite band.

August 23, 1988 - Scorpions bassist, Francis Buchholz. Savage Amusement Tour.

I would constantly listen to the interview, laughing at their innocence and wanting to become a rock star just like them. Later, I'd learn that Mama's Boys were going to be playing a show at the Ulster Hall. This was in April 1985, with F.M. opening as the supporting act. Denis and I bought tickets and could not contain our anticipation of going to what would be our first concert ever — The Power and Passion World Tour.

Scorpions rhythm / lead guitarist, Rudolph Schenker.

The concert was brilliant, but we were terrified, as it was rumored that during the song "Freedom Fighters," the divide we lived through was part of the show. We understood that Protestants in the audience would go to one side of the venue, Catholics to the other, and they would charge each other before meeting in the middle and getting into a full-blown war while the concert would play on.

Although this may have been a myth, it put us off at the end of the night once the show had wrapped up. As Pat, John, and Tommy did at the end of every gig, they announced they would be coming out into the foyer to meet fans and sign autographs. Denis and I chose to get back to the safety of our homes and left right after the show ended, not taking any chances

Scorpions vocalist, Klaus Meine.

for those who might be waiting for us. It was a dodgy time, and we were not about to find out if the war that didn't occur during the show would do so afterwards. Anyone who displayed their musical tastes on their denim and leather jackets, crombie coats, or blazers through metal buttons pinned or patched onto the fabric with needle and thread would often end up clashing on the bus.

Reading a band interview in a rock magazine called *Hit Parader*, none other than Scorpions drummer, Herman Rarebell.

After our move to Canada, my cousin Patrick told me he'd heard on the radio that my favourite band would be playing Winnipeg in September. He knew my passion for this group, as I had given him a loan of their self-titled album so he could see what their music was about. The frigger never did return it, stating that he had "misplaced it." Perhaps this was his way of payback for me using his parent's phone without their prior knowledge.

Upset by the fact that I never got my album back, I went ahead and bought a ticket for the show. I had no idea that this night would create a lifetime of memories and fond reflection, and would forever change my interaction with the music world.

It was Sunday, September 22, 1985, and the venue was called Le Rendezvous. Mama's Boys had a band in support called Labyrinth and another warm up act that I would only partly watch. I looked throughout the hall and noticed Tommy standing just outside the dressing room at the top of the stairs, watching the same act I was paying very little attention to. Since I had brought all my records to the show, I thought I would take a dander to the back of the hall and ask if Tommy would autograph them.

April 12, 1991 meeting Cinderella singer-songwriter, keyboardist, and guitarist, Tom Keifer.

When he came down, I explained that I had seen them play in Belfast just four months before and that I'd just moved to Canada. Tommy looked seemingly stunned to hear a wickedly thick Belfast brogue. He paused from autographing my albums, asked me to wait at the bottom of the stairs, ran up, and within moments he re-appeared and shouted, "C'mon up!"

I excused myself to the security guard who was standing half-way up the stairs and said, "Tommy McManus has invited me backstage." I am sure he had already realized that, but politeness sometimes goes a long way. This was an experience of a lifetime: meeting the musicians whose albums I constantly played on my brother's record player and got enough hidings from him for doing so.

When I first walked into the room I saw a white violin on a stand and recall saying, "My God, it's the Professor's fiddle." Then I saw Pat himself, who was working away on his Flying V. This guitar became a signature of his during band photo shoots. Tommy went back out to see the warm-up band play, as it was a passion of his to watch other acts onstage.

April 13, 1991. Cinderella bass guitarist, Eric Brittingham, and Tom Keifer, touring in support of their *Long Cold Winter* album.

There were two fellows in the room whom I did not immediately recognize. Regardless, I took a seat and started to talk with Pat, but sometime during the conversation I asked where John was. He replied, "He's sitting right next to you." When I turned to look, the first words out of my mouth were, "Jesus Christ, John. What happened to you? You look so different!"

Cinderella drummer, Fred Coury.

He was not wearing his signature item: a pair of rimless sunglasses (or his "bin lids" as John prefers to call them). Phil Lynott of Thin Lizzy fame had told them one night after they finished a gig that as a band, they had to dress differently from the fans. A big grin shot across Pat's face. From there on in the banter was brilliant.

As I sat and chatted between them, John offered me a beer. I asked him about his family and their beloved sister Valerie, who was tragically taken from them. I wanted to know everything about them, perhaps in my hopes of joining the band and touring the world with them. I went on to ask

Backstage post-concert waiting for an autograph from Slaughter drummer, Blas Elias.

about some of their songs, and during the conversation said, "Can you help me with the lyrics for the song 'One Last Chance'?" and did my very best to recite what I thought was correct and to the best of my knowledge.

John responded, "You know the words much better than I do," and burst into a fit of laughter. He never did tell me what the lyrics were.

Slaughter bassist, Dana Strum.

We spoke for ages before the lads had to tell me that it was time for them to get ready for the show. I went back downstairs, adrenaline rushing through my veins while trying to tell the group of lads whom I had been sitting with prior about my experiences in meeting Mama's Boys. They didn't have a clue what I was saying, but decided to look over my freshly autographed albums.

The fellows had writers' cramp that night. Even before they did their scheduled meet-and-greet session, I had them sign everything. Items included the outer record sleeves as well as the inner sleeve and the albums. They signed the inside of my leather jacket, a five dollar bill, the T-shirt and postergram

October 21, 1991 with Geoff Tate, vocalist for Queensrÿche, on their *Operation Mindcrime / Empire World Tour.*

they gave me, the back of my white granda shirt, and other picture disks I have including the 7" version of *Needle In The Groove* shaped like a three-leaf clover.

What was so incredible is that the lads fully obliged every signature. After this first time meeting a band, when I was a few years older I went on to interview other bands that came to town. Some of them found it to be a chore to sit down for a few minutes and give a few words or a photo. Many were fantastic and very approachable.

May 27, 2011 with Bono from U2 in Winnipeg as part of their 360° World Tour. I said to Bono, "Would you mind if a guy from Belfast got a picture with a guy from Dublin?"

U2, Cinderella, the Scorpions, Mötley Crüe, Slaughter, as well as individual artists from bands such as Anthrax, Queensrÿche, Metallica, AC/DC, Def Leppard, and Iron Maiden were great and down to earth. There were also those who were impossible to work with. And as much as I appreciate being in a band can be demanding, but, without a fan base and their support, many would not be able to maintain the status they have come to enjoy.

With the various bands that I have met or have worked directly for and with over the years, I've only come across a few who come close to the personalities of Pat, John, and Tommy. It's been twenty-eight years since I first met them, but it still sticks out in my mind as one of my greatest concerts and personal experiences. I was so hooked on their music and in wanting to be a part of the magic they created each and every night on stage. I wrote in the blurb beside my high school photo that I wanted to be a roadie for Mama's Boys. Sadly, much of this happiness would change.

May 17, 1992. Metallica vocalist and guitarist, James Hetfield. *Wherever We May Roam Tour.*

Metallica drummer, Lars Ulrich.

Tommy, who had been diagnosed with leukemia at the delicate age of nine, came out of remission and had a relapse. Although he came back to finish off the tour, he was soon admitted to hospital due to further complications from the disease. He fought additional battles over the years but remained committed to the band, following his childhood dream while inspiring millions the world over.

In 1987, I walked into a record shop in downtown Winnipeg and saw that they had released another album. The cover on both sides was shocking to say the least, as the record company had decided to mold the band to fit their defined image of what Mama's Boys should be and had added a fourth member. It changed everything. Who they were, the music they stood for, and what their sound and image meant to their fans. The album was a complete departure from what they had developed over the years as a distinct sound. No matter how many times I played the album, I struggled to get into it.

Unfortunately, the band lost a lot of impetus over the ensuing years, although I often longed for them to come back to Canada and would phone radio stations requesting their music be played without much success. I would still buy their earlier releases wherever I could find them, and I asked my mum to do the same for me when she took trips home.

April 13, 1991. Backstage with Slaughter guitarist, Tim Kelly. The band was touring in support of their debut album *Stick It To Ya* that also included their hit single, *Fly To The Angels*.

The band went through further line-up changes only to come full circle back to their roots, once again becoming the three-piece band they started out as and gained their greatest success with. I've often stated that those involved in the record company created much of the demise of Mama's Boys and should have the left the band alone. The old adage "If it ain't broke, don't fix it" should have been fully applied in this instance. I'd later learn that the last show Mama's Boys would ever play as the famous three brothers from Derrylin was on December 18, 1993, at the Fuchs Rain Hall in Mohlin, Switzerland.

In 1995, I decided to track the "Boys" down and see where they were and what they were doing. Constant phone calls led me to a DJ in Dublin. He told me that something tragic had happened to one of them. Not wanting to believe him, I went on a massive power search to find the truth. I finally reached their mother, Mrs. McManus at their family home, who shared with me what had happened.

## The Pulse of Derrylin

I sit here ready to write about,
Three young lads from Fermanagh I know.
Music they created when called Pulse,
Made many people's hearts glow.

These three lads that I speak about,
Started their careers quite young.
Playing the delicate music of Ireland,
At Fleadh Cheoils just for fun.

Suddenly all things in their careers would change,
Upon witnessing their first Horslips show.
The McManus brothers stood back in amazement,
When O'Connor played fiddle and bow.

The lads told their parents this show was so terrible,
They couldn't hear music, just noise.
Who'd ever guess that bearing witness to this,
Would form the Pulse of Mama's Boys.

Arriving home as they did at the end of each gig,
Their parents would ask the same.
If these shows are so terrible, so bad, and so boring,
How come you go every night in the rain?

Their names I can quote quite easily,
Tommy, John, and Pat The Professor.
Taking their lessons from the lads of Thin Lizzy,
And Horslips, Irish rock music's predecessor.

For John, the voice, the Uilleann pipes would not do,
Now he ran at a sprinter's pace.
His eyes locked upon his father so dear,
When he arrived home with the family's first bass.

Tommy, the bodhrán player, ever steady with the beat,
Was now also interested in new tunes.
His father decided it was time for some drums,
Instead of beating cushions with spoons.

Pat the Professor not to be forgotten,
Would prove he was a rising star.
Although he'd nick Johnny Fean's ideas,
He chose to play bow on guitar.

To the stage the brothers would take,
Singing songs derived from rock 'n' roll.
Adding Irish music to their newfound rhythms,
All the while playing from heart and soul.

Around the pubs in Ireland,
They toured themselves quite well.
Placing each fan in the crowd,
Under a euphoric spell.

To them it was never a problem,
How many fans came to the show.
As soon as the lights went down,
Mama's Boys were raring to go.

As a matter of fact,
It did not take long.
For their following to grow,
To hundreds and thousands strong.

For these brothers were very different,
In the way their music was played.
Always smiling while up on the stage,
Their faces never looking dismayed.

Over the days and throughout the years,
They sung out their songs with passion.
John learned while touring with Thin Lizzy,
That Phil Lynott's legwarmers were in fashion.

Sadly our happiness would suddenly change;
Tommy was called with a whisper in the breeze.
Fans found out that he was now drumming in heaven,
In sorrow, friends fell to their knees.

The rock world was stunned with this heartbreaking news,
Now the future for us all was uncertain.
Tommy made mention that if he were called to his maker,
With Phil Lynott he would draw a new curtain.

Looking down on us all, especially his family,
Tommy would not let this legacy come to an end.
His rhythm it beats within The Professor and John,
Now with Celtus, our hearts will mend.

★★★★★

At the incredibly young age of twenty-eight, on November 16, 1994, at 11:35pm, Thomas Gabriel McManus, drummer, background vocalist, and the driving force behind the band, passed away from complications three weeks after undergoing a bone marrow transplant for leukemia.

"Gentleman Rogues." John is in the background, with Tommy and I in the foreground. He is the reason I was inspired to become a drummer.

The news was devastating to the McManus family, and to friends, fans, and musicians around the world who knew and respected the work of these three brothers for their years of dedication to the music industry. The brilliance of musicianship as showcased by Mama's Boys had sadly and unexpectedly come to an end.

In 1995, I eventually caught up with John in a London studio and spoke to him for about forty-five minutes over the phone, recalling all of the events that had occurred. He mentioned that they were all still at a loss without Tommy, and that he and Pat did not know what the future held, as they could not look behind them knowing their beloved brother was not on the drums. His voice on the phone was understandably somber, although he took the time as they always did to answer my every question and was grateful for my phone call, no matter how painful it was.

In 1997, Pat and John reunited into a Celtic rock-based band called Celtus and released their first album called *Moonchild*, which is a haunting but very beautiful album. Tommy appears on this album through one of two tracks he last worked on: "Love Turns to Dust." It was because of this that I decided to compose a poem to the memory of Tommy, but also to thank the three of them for their brilliance in making one fan's dream come true as they did during two shows in 1985 and throughout their recording years.

For all the inspiration they gave me to realize my own dreams of perhaps becoming a musician one day, I felt it was the least I could do to capture their essence and preserve it forever in memory. Without question, they had already done this quite effortlessly through their music and dedication to their faithful followers.

When I was visiting family in Belfast in 1998, Celtus was scheduled to play the Point Depot in Dublin. I was hoping to get there either by train, car, or any other means, as I wanted to have the chance to catch up with John and Pat and speak to them at length about their journey of healing over the years after Tommy's untimely passing.

At that time I was told, as someone who'd never been to Dublin before or was there as a tourist, that thugs roamed the city and held hypodermic needles to the necks of any individuals who happened to wander into the wrong areas. They would be informed that the needle was loaded with a virus, before being stripped clean of their belongings. I didn't want to take any chances, and unfortunately never made it to the show. I was truly gutted by this.

In 2003, while on a trip back home, my Aunt Josephine, Uncle Thomas, and cousin Karl drove me down to Fermanagh to pay my respects to Tommy's grave. None of us knew where to find it, but as I had an address, we asked around. Eventually we ended up meeting with Mr. and Mrs. McManus, who were incredibly welcoming. I explained that I had written a composition about their famous sons and brought a copy with me to give to them. It was the first time I had shared this poem with anyone, but what an honour and privilege it was to stand in their cozy, welcoming home alongside Mr. McManus while listening to Mrs. McManus read aloud the piece I had written regarding their very talented and influential sons.

They brought us over to the grave and allowed me to take whatever time I needed to pay my respects to Tommy and his sister Valerie. I spent a good thirty minutes alone with them lost in thought and sadness as the gentleman who brought me backstage eighteen years earlier to meet his brothers and inspired me to become a drummer rested in peace beneath me.

Meeting John McManus on March 17th, 2011 in Belfast, before a Horslips concert.

I have since been home a number of times to catch Pat in concert, and have spent many hours sitting and recollecting with him and his lovely family, with his mum and dad and with Molly, who in 2009 brought me to my very first Horslips show. Pat has been as accommodating as always in signing my ever-expanding collection of Mama's Boys records, taking the time to look over the covers and note some he had never seen before. Although in one instance in 2006, at a concert and after autographing everything else in my collection, he signed my Official Bootleg album with "The signature remains the same."

On one of my last trips home in March of 2011, I met up with Molly and John before they headed off to attend another Horslips concert. This was a phenomenal reunion, as I had not seen John since 1985. The banter exchanged was fantastic, but I was shocked to see that I was now slightly taller than my childhood hero.

I can say that I am one amongst many who have truly been blessed with the friendships and welcoming hearts of the McManus family, as not only have they become wonderful friends over the years, but they have also become my family. Thank you all for the memories and for helping so many of us believe that we can pursue our dreams if we put our hearts and minds to it.

Tommy, I'm sure the concerts in heaven every night are sellouts alongside Phil Lynott, Gary Moore, Rory Gallagher, and Kurt Cobain. Save us a seat in the front row. And as your dear sister Molly always tells me while pumping her fists in the air: keep rockin'!

★★★★★

Since writing this personal reflection and poem, a beautiful man who made me so incredibly welcome every time I went back to Ireland, a man who spoke so dearly about his sons that remain legendary musicians and inspirations to this day, peacefully passed away on my mum's birthday of May 3, 2013. Although I could not make it home for the funeral service, I was with you all in spirit. Thus, I would like to dedicate this reflection and poem to the beloved memory of John McManus, Sr., and to his children Tommy and Valerie McManus. I'm sure you are enjoying spending quality time together again now that you have all been reunited, but are also remaining watchful

**This picture was taken on my fourth trip home in 2006, whereby I called in to visit Mr. and Mrs. John and Valerie McManus, who have made me most welcome every time I've called around.**

over your loved ones left behind to cherish your wonderful memories and all you gave to this world. We have been enriched by your gifts of love, kindness, and friendship.

My love to you all…

## Mum's Lament

ONE OF THE most difficult days I have ever faced in my life was when I had to say goodbye one last time to our family matriarch, my Mum: Catherine Philomena McVicker (nee Devlin). She was a warrior in her own right who fought for her beliefs and for the protection of her children. She watched over us by day and by night and raised us with good intentions, only wanting to see the best for us. She put her family ahead of herself and fought a courageous battle against a silent killer.

Having grown up in war-torn Northern Ireland, my father could not find work at home and spent his entire life at sea. He worked hard to provide a pay packet that he would send home to my mum, and from which she balanced a mortgage, bought supplies, kept a roof over our heads,

Along with our beloved mum, my brother and me saying it all with the shirts we were wearing! This was taken on my twenty-first birthday. Four days later would be our sixth year in Canada.

took care of the garden, drove four kids to countless doctor's appointments, met with teachers, ran errands, did laundry, cooked meals, and cleaned a house. She had many other wonderful attributes and did so much more while asking for nothing in return.

She made sure our Christmas celebrations and Easters were filled with joy and made our birthdays incredibly special while fully celebrating our successes in life. She picked us up from our failings and helped us through the lessons learned from those. She nurtured and cherished her family to no end and did everything to protect us from the violence that surrounded us in Belfast.

It was in January of 2005 that complications from her illness started to make their presence quite well known within my mum. Prior to leaving for Belfast in February of 2005, as my uncle had just passed away, my mum told me that she and my dad would need me back in Canada to help them. I stressed that I would be back but did not read between the lines of what she was going through. It was tough to see her struggle for breath and be placed on oxygen a few days prior on January 31, for she gave her four asthmatic children the breath of life. She made sure that we had the necessary medicines required so that we ourselves could breathe while growing up in the damp Irish climate. With her strong will, strong mind, and inconceivable determination, she fought like a warrior against this disease.

Thirty-six hours after we had laid his father to rest, my cousin Stephen was murdered. Having to break the news to my parents would not be easy, as I did not want to place further stress on my mum due to her breathing difficulties. Upon hearing the long-distance rings at four o'clock in the morning, and although my dad took the call, she knew something was wrong and came to the phone. It was my duty to tell her, so I asked her to please sit down first. I explained that I would have to stay home a little longer and deal with a second and completely unexpected death. I had left my university studies in early February to attend one funeral and represent our family since my mum was not able to go. I returned to Canada completely wrecked and shattered after having to attend a second burial.

After being back for a few months, it was around 7:10pm on the evening of Sunday, April 17, and while visiting my mum who was staying at a unit for patients living with Chronic Obstructive Pulmonary Disease, her first words laid me flat out as if I had been sucker punched.

"Greg love, I'm terminal."

The shock and disbelief were incomprehensible to my heart and mind. Why did I not know sooner? Why was this happening? What did I do to deserve yet another blow? Why was life being so bloody cruel? The questions were endless.

I walked out into the hallway and paced a number of circles, not knowing how to take the news my mum had shared with me only seconds before. I had no idea she was that far advanced with her illness. Panicking, I went back to ask her if this was true? Was she having me on? How long would she have to live? I asked a multitude of other questions that people ask when they find out their loved one is literally dying right before their own two eyes. She tried to reassure me that the specialists who work with this disease were well on top of things, and that she would likely have twenty to thirty years still in front of her. She did this to try and set my heart and mind at ease, as she knew the questions I asked provided completely different answers from those she was telling me. The shock from this news was overwhelming. I needed to know more about it.

Upon getting home later that night, I researched everything I possibly could about this disease. The results that came back did not add comfort. From what I read with the onset of Idiopathic Pulmonary Fibrosis, I learned that Idiopathic meant "of unknown origin" and that a person who has been diagnosed with this disease has approximately ten years to live. However, with the onset of oxygen, a person has their lifespan reduced to five years, although the outcome on average is two years and eight months.

My mum was in a unit for persons learning how to live with Chronic Obstructive Pulmonary Disease yet to my understanding, her diagnosis was the complete opposite of this. She had been on oxygen for three months, so I believed we would have at least another two-and-a-half years to fully enjoy our time with her and do everything in life that we never had the time to do. I wanted to spend every waking minute telling her how much we loved her and cherished all the wonderful things she had done for us over the years. I wanted her to know how grateful I was to her for having the gut wrenching courage to leave her own mother, sisters, and brother behind to create new opportunities for her children.

We are never told in advance what our time allotment in life is. So much for the average timeframe I had researched online. Twenty-six days after she had first broken the news to me, and on the afternoon of Wednesday, May 11, 2005 at 3:49:48 in the afternoon, we said one last goodbye to the woman who had given us everything and left us begging for nothing. My mum joined her parents, sisters, and brothers on the other side in the spirit world.

Just before she passed, and while I stood over her in her hospital bed, I said, "Mum, I love you" four times in succession. My heart and soul literally died when she mustered up every ounce of energy to repeat those words back to me while taking her last breaths in life, surrounded by sixteen loving family members. The grief, sadness, and despair that accompanied this, was overwhelming as her passing also impacted the nurses who had provided care for her.

I guess I somehow knew the time was coming. A week before, while sitting on my bed, I saw my grandparents and my mum's two brothers standing at the foot of it. I did not welcome their presence with open arms, but demanded to know why they were there. I was defiant and told them they were not taking my beloved mum. As much as I appreciated seeing them, I shouted that it was not her turn and asked for them go back to where they came from.

I really did not have a choice, for they came to release her from her suffering and let me know that I needed to prepare. My protests did not account for anything, and it would not have been fair to my mum to prolong her suffering. Who was I to question why it was her time to venture into new beginnings, a new life, a new adventure?

Some of my mum's last words to me before she passed were, "Greg, I'm not getting out of this hospital. I'm not coming home." I reassured her that she was coming home and that she would indeed be in her house again. Little did I realize that my words would be true: we brought her back for her wake to celebrate her beautiful and courageous life under the cloak of death.

The wake and all other events associated with her passing are a complete blur in my mind, yet everything remains so clear. Family and friends came from all over the world to participate in the celebration of my mum's life, lifting a toast over her while saying words that captured the spirit of who she was and what she stood for.

She looked very beautiful and very peaceful in her casket, and she was no longer hooked up to a machine that provided her with assistance in breathing. But nothing could ever bring her back, no matter how much our hearts broke, our minds wished, and our prayers asked. She was free to embark upon a new journey.

On the morning of May 16, my mum would be leaving her family home for the last time and heading on to the church for final service before internment at the chosen cemetery. It was around 4:00am when I sat down in front of the computer at my parent's house, my mum only a matter of steps away from me, and composed this lament to her memory. It took two hours to write, and I asked my dad, Karen, Joe, and Ange to review it and see what they thought. I sought their approval as every poem I've ever written was reviewed and edited by my mum, with the exceptions of "Lament for a Child," "The Confessional," "Bruised and Battered," and "Disposable Human," as they are recent compositions. She would provide guidance when I was constructing each piece and would give me the background for those I was unsure about, such as Knockagh Monument being a war memorial.

I asked my dad and siblings to sign one copy of the composition before placing it in with my mum. From there, I simply lay on the floor below her casket, facing her, wanting to have my time alone with her. I knew it would be the last chance I would get, as she was leaving for the church at 11:00am for her final service.

I had faced her in a similar manner the day before she passed away, sneaking back to the hospital around 10:00pm and putting my head on her pillow only inches from her face to breathe with her for over two hours. She gave me the gift of life and breath, and I wanted to share that gift with her one more time. It was difficult to breathe at her slow pace. I had less than thirty-five years with my mum, a lifetime far too short but wanted to take every moment afforded to me.

The church was packed, and the service beautiful. She was surrounded by the warmth and love that she herself had given to countless people over her years. I explained to those gathered about the development of "Whispers in the Breeze," the eulogy to my mum and composition as written that very morning. There was not a dry eye among those in attendance, as somehow while choking back tears and trying to maintain a little of the same composure she did when speaking from her heart about my Aunt Sadie, I managed to read both pieces to my mum's honour and memory.

Coming down from the altar, I placed my hand on the church cloth that blanketed my mum's casket before placing one final kiss to where I knew her head lay. I did not want to let go. It was hard to have to say goodbye, but we had to get through this for her.

At the site of internment we gave out forty roses: twenty-eight red for the adults and twelve white for the grandchildren and children who were a part of my mum's life, including one to a little girl who was named after her. Kathleen Lebel. Her mother, Tara Cahill, had honoured my mum by naming her daughter after her. This extremely beautiful gesture forever left a unique mark on us all. Tara and my mum had a special relationship in all their years of working together. Tara, you may not know this: my mum always considered and counted you as one of her own children, along with Rosemary Henderson. All of you are an amazing part of our family, for which we are truly blessed.

Upon lowering my mum down to her final resting place, I asked those in attendance to follow us in our Irish traditions and to take a handful of soil and place it on her casket so we could start our burial process. With the soil in my hand and while looking down where she lay beneath me, I started by saying, "Mna na hÉireann, mo mháthair, mo chroí, tá tú go hálainn. Go n-éirí an t-ádh leat agus go mbeannaí Dia dhuit, Mum." This means, "Woman of Ireland, my mother, my love, you are beautiful. Good luck and God bless, Mum."

My beautiful mum, Catherine McVicker, who unselfishly gave everything of herself to raise and protect her family in a country torn by political war, and religious persecution. She is the reason I was inspired to write this book.

I'm sure she would have been so proud of how we brought her through her final moments in life with us before we laid her to eternal rest. I watched and learned from her putting her own family members to rest over the years and tried to follow those teachings with the same dignity she gave to everyone else.

It has been almost nine years since we said goodbye to the loving woman who was our mother, a beautiful wife, a dedicated sister, an amazing granny, and all the other wonderful things she stood for. Although never forgotten, we often reflect upon things that are special within our hearts, especially those times we spent with her. She was truly the nucleus of our family.

Mum, I want you to know that your love, your memories, and your wisdom, will forever carry on within each one of us. This poem and entire book is dedicated to the love and memory of Catherine McVicker, who was one incredibly awesome lady for her courage, perseverance, guidance, dedication, and protection of her four children, as only a mother knows how to do.

## Mum's Lament

Our mother's love so special,
As many folks can see.
Mum's greatest gift was giving life,
To my sisters, brother, and me.

We began as children so helpless, Mum,
Yet never a challenge for you.
No matter how little or large the task,
There's nothing you couldn't do.

Throughout the years and as we grew,
So proud of us you were.
If we needed something, Mum,
We knew you'd always be there.

You gave us so much precious love,
Which came from deep inside.
Knowing the amazing Mum you are,
Fills us with tremendous pride.

You steered us through our battles, Mum,
No one can disagree.
You guided us in darkened times,
And now we set you free.

You taught us so much wisdom, Mum,
And loved us with your heart.
A new journey you shall now begin,
For a little while we must part.

Mum, our time with you was far too short,
There's much we'd like to say.
The days ahead they are unknown,
Without you leading the way.

Although you'll look down upon us, Mum,
And incredibly sad, we'll fuss.
We take great pride in the fact that,
Your blood flows proudly through us.

Mum, we share your strengths instilled in us,
Knowing what we must do.
To continue the legacy you've already begun,
While lovingly remembering you.

Sail gently into the night, our love,
Your new beginning has come.
Although at this moment we say farewell,
Forever you are our Mum.

A wee message from Daddy too:
Kathleen, my sweet precious angel, a loving mum.
Tiocfaidh Ár Lá,
(Our day will come).

Mum, Dad is our sailor, you are our captain and ship,
And we, your children, are your crew.
With everlasting love and fondest memories until we meet again,
Karen, Joseph, Gregory, and Angela.
Go n-éirí an t-ádh leat agus go mbeannaí Dia dhuit, Mum.
(Good luck and God bless).

★★★★★

Friends familiar with this chapter of my life asked, "How did you get through this period?" They recognized that within a three-month timeframe, I had undergone the death of an uncle, the murder of my cousin, and returned to Canada only to find out my mum was terminal.

The answer to how I overcame all of this is not a simple one. I had to realize my purpose in life. It was not going to be an easy journey but I needed to start with a lot of healing. I took a risk against the advice of the priest who presided over my mum's service. He'd asked me to not enter into four sweat lodge ceremonies, as the stress I was facing and the consequence of trying to do too much could have grave outcomes for me. As much as I appreciated his concern, I continued with my university studies and met with Elder Garry "Morning Star" Raven.

Just like my mum did for all of those years while growing up in Belfast, Elder Raven took me under his wing for a while after learning about the traumas I had experienced. But I would have to learn how to stand on my own two feet, as I no longer had my mum to turn to for advice when faced with difficult life decisions.

## From a Child to the Man

WHEN I FIRST immigrated in 1985, I really had no interest in school and learning the same educational processes that I had already undergone in Belfast. Not purposely trying to knock another country's systems, but the education back home was far more advanced than that of Canada. I had one year left of school but would have to undergo a number of courses and three additional years to capture a Grade Twelve education.

I resented this fact, along with suffering tremendous homesickness. Although I made the daily shuffle to Churchill High School, I did not bother applying myself in any aspect whatsoever. History was the one subject area I completely despised, since my history background was steeped in Britain and Europe, even as far back as the Vikings and the Normandy invasions.

I knew nothing of this country. I wanted to go home to the land I loved, to the friends I knew, and to the life I was asked to leave behind, which is not easy to do at fifteen years of age.

It was different for Karen and Joe, as they had already finished grammar school and were working. They were quite happy to leave Northern Ireland behind due to the traumas they suffered while going to school and in our once peaceful neighbourhood, which became filled with much of the same taunting and bitterness. They often asked why I longed to go home.

It was a day in 1986, and the class I was to attend was called History 200. However, this fateful day only cemented my thoughts that I definitely would not learn about this country while under rules of imposed reading. Instruction had been given to the class. I sat at my desk, lost within my own thoughts and without even opening my textbook. The teacher came by and, in an infuriated state, opened the red-covered textbook in front of me with the word CANADA blazing across the top. He pushed my head into it and demanded I start reading.

I sat there momentarily while reflecting on what had just happened. Images and text of the Fur Trade peered out of the pages back at me. We had been punished to no end by corporal school laws, strapped at every opportunity our bastard teachers could find to leave our hands stinging and our tears flowing. This country where such a barbaric practice was supposedly outlawed suddenly came into question for me.

I closed the textbook, threw everything into my bag, and walked out of the classroom. Although the teacher had locked the door behind me (as he did to other students who were late for his class), I never went back. On the scheduled times I was supposed to be there for the remainder of the year, I would hang out with mates, walk to the local 7-11, go to the gym, or sit in the computer class. I learned nothing about Canada that year, and needless to say, I failed the course.

My understanding came through reading newspapers and listening to conversations, but this was more about the political landscape than history. My mind was not skewed by documents written predominantly by colonizers who sought to eradicate the truths about how the country itself was founded. I had a unique respect for aboriginal people, specifically First Nations, who also self-identify as Indians.

I had seen through my own eyes the remnants of many First Nations who frequented the downtown core of Winnipeg.

Substance misuse was rampant among those living on the street, although the word "living" is quite a generous one – barely surviving would be a more accurate reflection. One has only to take a few courses in Native Studies to understand why so many of these beautiful people have ended up kicked beyond the curb and into the gutter of life, ostracized largely by the dominant society. Imposed tactics of colonization and the effects of these archaic methods ripple rampantly today, as do biases and racist views that persist and saturate much of people's viewpoints against First Nations, their practices, languages, traditions, and spiritual beliefs.

Prior to starting my university studies, I read about the shooting death of the First Nations leader J.J. Harper back on March 9, 1988. He was killed by a Winnipeg police officer, which intrigued me to want to learn more. And so in my first year of post secondary education, I took a few courses in Native Studies, the first in September of 2004 entitled "The Native Peoples of Canada – Part One," from which I was enthralled and enraged at what our professor shared with us. It was through his teachings that I wrote my first letter to the editor at one of Canada's largest newspapers, expressing how outraged I was at how Aboriginal veterans, who had freely volunteered their time and laid down their lives for this county during World War I and II, were treated upon their return. Racist policies had been developed that excluded them from receiving the same rights, recognition, and benefits as others, including five acres of land for farming.

My professor had spent a lifetime working with First Nations and Inuit communities, and obviously his passion instilled a raging inferno within me. Not all of his students agreed with my passion. I heard racially prejudiced overtones and views by another student whose father was also a police officer, and had held the same hatred and bigoted views against Aboriginal people as I had seen back home by our own police force against Irish Catholics. I was hungry to enrich my knowledge, while learning the dark secrets of this country in its efforts to assimilate "the Indian within" while wiping out its Indigenous population. I was not really surprised to learn this though, as the last Indian Residential School closed in 1996 in the province of Saskatchewan.

It was May 24, 2005, and thirteen days after my beloved mum had passed away, yet only eight days since we had laid her to rest. I'd decided I would continue with my studies, and I sat at the right side of the classroom, lost in my grief. While listening to the instructor, we were informed that an Elder would be joining us to share his experiences. This included his expectations of us as students, as we would first be embarking upon five days of classroom instruction, then five days of living within a First Nations community and participating in many traditional ceremonies and cultural practices.

On day two, Elder Raven made his presence felt within the classroom, and we were asked to push all desks aside and to form our chairs into what I would later come to understand as a sharing circle. His face was soft and kind, but rough from his experiences in the system. His black and silver hair was tied in two braids, which rested upon each shoulder.

Elder Raven openly disclosed that he did not make it past grade three due to the deplorable actions of those who were sent to "remove the savage from within." I often wondered who the true savages were, from their despicable actions of human destruction, to their ability to live with their draconian views and the implementation of them.

He spoke eloquently, but while tuned in to his comments I was also trying to formulate my own thoughts and wonder how I was to speak to a classroom full of fellow students who were complete strangers to me. How was I to share exactly what I was feeling at that moment, drowning in a complete abyss of sorrow at having lost my mum? Could I control my emotions, or was I so grief-stricken that I would not make sense to anyone? My nerves were extremely raw at this point, so who knew what I was going to say.

My comments ended up simply coming from the heart, as there was no way that I could possibly string together a few sentences about what I expected or hoped to gain from this class or from the sharing circle. I introduced myself and explained that my mum, my best friend, my guide in life and realistically my guardian angel, had passed away. I also explained the events of February: my uncle died, and within thirty-six hours of his burial, his son was brutally murdered. I explained that I was with my cousin that night and was supposed to go back out with him for a couple of pints, but he had decided to take time alone to grieve the passing of his father. I shared that I had last seen Stephen at 9:30pm, and that within a matter of six hours, as gale force winds howled on a cold, bitter night through the streets of Belfast, he was taking his final breaths.

With all of these traumas, I explained that I simply wanted to follow my mum into the grave. My spirit was completely shattered, and I had lost the will to live. There was nothing left of me other than that of a broken human being. My hope from the sharing circle and Elder Raven was that they would restore my spirit and my belief. Even the unbiased, forgiving, nurturing love provided to me freely on a daily basis by my two beautiful children, was not enough to keep my spirit alive. I was dead inside and felt that the only other alternative was to leave the physical world behind and join my mum in the spirit world.

I honestly have no idea what anyone else said that day, their expectations, what they hoped to gain from the course or from any experiences that would occur while living within the community for the short period of time that we were to be there. Although, there were a few who seemingly understood where I was coming from and how my life had completely changed on May 11, as they themselves had gone through some very personal losses.

I was lost within the depths of my own grief, a very dark and lonely place to be. This made it difficult to relate to anyone. I was determined to go to the community to heal, pray, and seek guidance. I wanted to find my soul and my very being in order to make some sense of life and what it all meant. This was not going to be an easy feat, but somehow, likely from the guidance and love my mum had instilled within me over the years, I found the strength and encouragement I needed to do this.

The first five days in the classroom came and went in an instant. I completed the work assigned to me. I had spent the weekend buying cloth, ribbon, tobacco, food, and supplies while preparing for the unexpected. I had never set foot in a First Nations community before, which is also referred to as a reserve.

We left in groups the following Monday morning and were greeted by Morning Star at his place of residence. Mother Earth. The presence of warmth, sharing, and guidance, as well as the seven sacred teachings—love, respect, humility, courage, honesty, truth, and wisdom—surrounded us, but in the face of my overwhelming grief it was easy to lose sight of this.

The landscape was something none of us were accustomed to. Reserves in Manitoba are nothing to be proud of. The conditions in which these loving people have been forced to live are akin in many instances to those of third world countries, and are extremely deplorable.

Elder Raven brought us into his home and shared with us teachings of the medicine wheel, giving us many aspects other than those customarily taught. He helped us understand how the teachings applied to us, and how we are all one in this world regardless of the differences and biases that separate us. He did not reference this but in my opinion, the economic imbalances as seen throughout his community by my observations left me wondering if I was still in Canada.

We had to work together as a group to construct the tipis in which we would sleep. We had to help gather firewood to keep us warm at night as we slept under the watchful eyes of the Creator, and prepared food we would eat as a family while learning the spiritual and traditional ways of Elder Raven's people. We would also learn what to expect within the sweat lodge, the sharing circle within a tipi, as well as within a healing circle, and how to prepare for these sacred and beautiful ceremonies.

I was determined to do four sweats that week, the first dedicated to the memory of my mum, the second for my uncle and cousin, the third for the love of my children, and the fourth for myself. As the conductor of each sweat, Elder Raven and the other participants listened as I poured out my heart within the sanctuary and safety of the sacred lodge and sharing circles. I listened to the teachings along with traditional songs, while drums and rattles were played. It was a spiritual journey of profound reflection. Elder Raven allowed me to find myself. He also helped me to heal my shattered spirit. This healing process was shared with those who at first were complete strangers to me in a classroom but over a five-day period, they became part of a family unit within the confines of a small First Nations community.

In August of 2005, upon my return, I participated in another four sweats, one of which was a warrior sweat. This intense spiritual journey was like no other I had ever experienced. To have been proclaimed a warrior by those who gave me the strength to live after the death of my mum, and who welcomed me into their community without a notion of my being and without any preconceived biases, is something I will always be truly grateful for. They helped me seek out the guidance I needed to look at the gift of life I have been given, and to cherish each new day.

Am I completely healed from all of the heartbreaking events that occurred in 2005? I will say no, I am not. A journey of healing cannot be captured within a predetermined timeframe. I still miss my mum everyday and would do anything to be able to hear her voice again, to wrap my arms around and give her a hug, or to understand and listen to her brilliance and profound ability to recollect dates and times from her life growing up in Belfast.

I would love to hear her wit, humour, craic, and banter; to hear her sing songs of years gone by from her own childhood days; to hear her say "Gregory" in the way that she did, or to simply hear her say "I love you" one more time.

There will come a day when I will see you again, Mum, and the reunification will be a Céilí that the spirit world has never seen before. Thank you for all of your sacrifices and for the courage and strength required to move your family to a place where they could prosper, a place without the hatred you tried to protect us from every day in our young lives.

I love you and miss you, and only the Creator knows how much my heart breaks every day.

Imagine That

MANY HEADLINE IMAGES splashed across our television screens make worldwide news but eventually fade to black and are replaced with the next breaking news segment.

We are no longer informed of the events that are occurring in Port-au-Prince unless the media decides to provide us with a yearly update. We are left wondering whether people are still starving or if efforts of aid got into the hands of every person who required it. Did the survivors rebuild their lives, or have we become immune to the disparities people faced? Because we were informed through the media that aid and government assistance was provided to those in need, should we be happy with that? Rarely have I ever seen much follow-up to this story. The same can be said for the Japan tsunami, unless there is an update on radiation leaks or debris floating across the Pacific Ocean.

Headlines shifted focus to Pakistan and India due to severe flooding and to the loss and displacement of life, along with massive uprisings and slayings of people within the Middle East in areas such as Libya, and in Tahrir Square in Egypt. Then we learned that twenty innocent children and six teachers in Newton, Connecticut, were gunned down, the Boston Marathon was bombed, and Oklahoma City was hit by several tornadoes. The world learned about the alleged usage of chemical weapons on innocent people in Syria. Now, a monumental disaster is unfolding throughout the Philippines as a result of the category

5, Super Typhoon Haiyan, and in Tacloban, which some survivors who struggle to find food and clean water, have labeled as the "city of the living dead". But, how long do we stay attuned to these events, before moving on to the next natural, man-made disaster, or act of global terrorism? Are we defined in life by the latest news headlines?

There is so much that still goes on in this world today that does not make much sense. Apparently equality for women is on the rise (but nowhere near satisfactory), yet the practice of female genital mutilation still occurs in some cultures. Recent events in Canada concerned honour killings, which claimed the lives of four female relatives from one family. Would someone please explain what is honourable about killing another human being, regardless of whether they are your family or an enemy?

How is it that the world's richest countries can spend billions on destructive weapons, yet at the same time, health care is only provided to those who can afford it? And as seen in the housing market crisis in 2009, why are bank executives, who willingly destructed the lives of millions of people and destroyed thousands of dreams due to their own greed, still afforded lucrative bonuses and provided immunity from prosecution?

Explain why millionaires who are spoiled by the riches of seemingly never-ending dollars made on the backs of other people are comfortable while world poverty still exists without rhyme or reason.

Why is it that can we fly humans into space (including the most recent and very successful journey whereby we were amazed and enthralled by powerful images provided to us from the stars beyond through social media by Canadian astronaut Chris Hadfield), yet diseases such as malaria, cholera, HIV, and tuberculosis are pervasive in many poor nations, as well as some wealthy, while pharmaceutical companies continue to make billions of dollars?

Why do child labour sweatshops in other countries often have a blind eye turned towards them? Why do factories get built to the poorest standards possible, with people expected to work eighteen hours a day or not get the dollar promised?

Social constructs have obviously failed us, for who are we to create laws and policies that empower some and despair others? There is something wrong with all of these pictures yet these are all real life occurrences.

As a result, I've often wondered what the world might look like if everything we did was completely opposite from what we as humans have become accustomed to.

## Imagine That...

Imagine that you wake up from a dream,
Only to find you are still asleep.
That you believe you are in shallow water,
When it's actually over ten feet.

Imagine that your television is your only friend,
To whom you can always talk.
That the wheelchair in which you sit,
Provides you with the legs to walk.

Imagine that the trigger of the gun you fire,
Will call upon world peace.
That the last payment on your new car,
Is just the start of its lease.

Imagine that when you arrive at work,
You are always sent home with pay.
That you are a motivational speaker,
But do not know what to say.

Imagine that the sun went down,
Although there was always light to shine.
That all forms of money went obsolete,
Yet payphones still required a dime.

Imagine that we were all created equal,
But to each other we were not the same.
That we all went through the journey of life,
Confident in playing the game.

Imagine that you reached your destination,
Yet you haven't boarded the plane.
That you are released from the padded room,
When the white coats know you're insane.

Imagine that when a bank is robbed,
The thieves put the money in the vault.
That with each performed abortion,
The child is born without fault.

Imagine that with the money you've spent,
All of your purchases are free.
That if these words I write were true,
What kind of a world this would be.

## C'est La Vie

"THAT'S LIFE." I began reflecting on the things in life we want to do and create bucket lists, but find many challenges block our way. I wondered if there is a reason? Is it a fear of not knowing that we can accomplish things that we put our minds to? Is it a fear of the unknown? Or is it that we do not believe in ourselves and create barriers to hold us back from achieving our goals?

Oftentimes and in trying to assure those around us, we will make statements completely opposite to how we are truly feeling. Is this a human trait, trying to shield others from our pain? Or are we simply trying to ignore the truth so as to not have to open up to someone else around us? When heartbroken from a relationship and people know we are grieving the loss, we try to let others know we are fine. But deep down inside, our stomachs are in knots, headaches abound, and we feel awful. They see this, but we try to mask our feelings in order to protect those who are worried about our wellbeing. Why do we do this? What purpose does it serve?

As beautiful as the creation of life itself is, we as humans have never been provided with an instruction manual as to how to go through complexities of life, communicate in the absence of language, sort our feelings, or live within the definition of being human (as no one can tell us what the proper way of being one is).

We create differing levels of society and try to impose our belief systems onto other cultures by telling them that in order to be human, they have to be more like us. Who are we to dictate the creation of life when we ourselves are not perfect? It's easy to say treat all humans equally and be kind to one another, but that has never been the case.

## C'est La Vie

Have you ever tried to shout out loud,
But you have forgotten how to scream.
Have you ever tried to fall asleep,
When you are already in a dream.

Have you ever tried to run away,
But you have no idea how to walk.
Have you ever tried to have a conversation,
When you know not how to talk.

Have you ever tried to read a book,
But you have lost your sense of sight.
Have you ever tried to climb a mountain,
When you know your fear of height.

Have you ever wanted to visit your past,
But you have no clue where you've been.
Have you ever tried to hide your face,
When you're crowned a beauty queen.

Have you ever tried to stop the bleeding,
But you never received a cut.
Have you ever wanted to lie down and die,
When your coffin has already been shut.

Have you ever tried to place a wager,
But you haven't a penny to bet.
Have you ever tried to love someone,
When you've never even met.

Have you ever looked at yourself in a mirror,
But don't recognize what you see.
Have you ever tried to say you're fine,
When your body is in agony.

Have you ever tried to have a laugh,
But all you ever do is cry.
Have you ever tried to kiss the moon,
When you have no wings to fly.

Have you ever wanted to change the world,
But you don't know what it should be.
Have you never realized that these things happen for a reason,
When the truth is c'est la vie.

# Taking a Stand

A S A STUDENT in the faculty of social work, learning about systems theories, behavioural theories, and feminist perspectives, I found my time as an earnest learner to become severely skewed one day. The reason was that a tragic event had occurred eighteen years earlier and was now being recognized. This compelled me to start writing articles that addressed human injustices in an effort to raise social awareness and to try to change social policy.

It was on December 6, 1989, that fourteen women, all of whom were engineering students, were gunned down at École Polytechnique de Montréal. After separating female from male students, the gunman shouted, "I hate feminists!" before opening fire. In their efforts to better their education, personal lives, and society, fourteen women were murdered.

I asked why on a day of national mourning, and one in which the Parliament of Canada lowered all flags to half-mast, why only five people from campus could find the time to gather at University Centre to recognize, remember, and reflect upon a day that took those lives? We were like those students in Montreal, coming from all walks of life to gain a post-secondary education. As such, I thought that my own university should have a policy written that dedicated time to attend and reflect upon such tragic events. In an institution that had 5,000 faculty and staff and over 26,000 students, by my own count, less than sixty people attended the memorial services and speeches given. I pondered aloud if as a society we had simply become complacent?

For those who made up the breadth of our institution, whether they were in administration, deans of various faculties, professors, instructors, or students, I struggled to understand why so little emphasis and awareness was associated with this day of remembrance. I asked myself if this was the value we placed on women in society. Are we, who live in a county as rich as Canada, cognizant that we uphold patriarchal belief systems and structures?

During my years of study, women in the Canadian workforce were met with glass ceilings and only made seventy-three cents to every dollar their male counterparts made, yet their efforts and education were the same. I had to ask: are we just ignorant because the shootings did not happen here? Or are woman seen as being less than equal in society and this is an acceptable standard? Sorry, but not in my worldview.

I looked on as the Womyn's Centre recreated the aftermath of events that surrounded that unforgettable day. Female students volunteered to lay their still bodies upon the dusty floor of University Centre, symbolizing those women who met untimely, horrendous fates. A female violinist played a mournful song as another young woman with chalk in hand drew an outline around each student who so bravely recounted the aftermath of that tragic day.

The date does not change, nor will the events of that day be eradicated from history. However, it was overheard from patrons in line at the coffee shop next to these women that, "They must be from the arts department, recreating a drama or play." Excuse me? Eighteen years later, can we willfully forget about the fourteen women who died and the additional thirteen people injured in an institution such as the one I was attending? Did people simply add their own perspectives and think that as it did not happen in Winnipeg, we need not worry about what had happened two provinces away? Out of sight, out of mind perhaps?

Regardless of this, I was one of three males who took in this event and observed in silence as one woman photographed the portrayal of this appalling day, reminiscent of the work crime scene detectives would have done.

While taking the feminist perspectives course, a privilege wheel was presented by our instructor that addressed opportunity, advantage, and benefits among people that are white, straight, married, able bodied, Christian, educated, and employed English-speaking males who are healthy, have children, and are homeowners between the ages of 30-45. They are granted greater privileges and recognition in society, while those on the outside considered to be part of the fringe are marginalized and/or oppressed. I challenged this and conceived my own term with respect to feminism, although this does not mean I take the same perspective of the gunman and "hate feminists."

As a "femanist," I welcomed feminist theories, as they challenged my views and enhanced my role of advocating for women's rights so that women are afforded equal opportunity, status, benefits, rights, and pay. Additionally, a "femanist" is any person who, regardless of their gender or sexual orientation, challenges the status quo by seeking to end all practices of oppression and domination towards each and every individual by incorporating holistic practices and through the creation of equality for all humanity. Not everyone follows ideals presented by the privilege wheel. My fellow male classmates held similar views to those of my own.

It was felt that the position these women held in society was made up of traditional roles: staying home to cook and clean, raise children, be complacent in their everyday lives, and provide conjugal enjoyment for their male partners. These views could not have been further from the truth, but often reflect a value associated with women in Canadian society and throughout the world.

I believe members of society who identify as feminists, "femanists," students, and the institutions they attend, that we all need to finally come together as a collective unit and stand tall while respectfully remembering and reflecting upon the estimated six hundred Aboriginal women who have disappeared across Canada, the countless numbers of women who have become victims of violence, and the fourteen women who were murdered at École Polytechnique de Montréal.

Although long overdue, the time has come for us to take a stand and advocate for change.

## Alcohol Saviour

I N MY FORMER career, I came across a lady who was panic-stricken, as her house was not in order before I arrived to complete the work requested of me. I assured her that I was not there to judge or question, but was there to provide the services she had ordered.

She was eager to share her life story. Someone to tell, and no matter how agonizing it was, she needed to get her story of her chest. She chose a complete stranger whom she would never see again, and without knowing if judgment would be cast after leaving. She did not want a professional who set a sixty-minute time limit while charging a large sum of money for merely listening and asking questions such as, "How did that make you feel?"

A professional by trade, she had an insatiable thirst for alcohol as soon as her shift ended. Dropping her entire paycheque at the bar in one night was not uncommon. Credit cards became another choice of payment, but that was soon shut down due to uncontrollable spending at the bar and entering into debt during one binge period. As a result, she would frequent payday loan companies in advance of her bi-weekly paycheque as the next method to secure money for drink. The last method was through supposed "friends."

The mass consumption of drink was not due to her being an alcoholic. This was used as a coping mechanism to block out painful events after large amounts of liquor were inhaled. Men, who passed themselves off as being her friends, would help fuel the liquid inferno within her soul before degrading all aspects of her dignity.

She explained that there was usually more than one involved in the savage events that occurred each time. She went on to say that some believed her addiction to alcohol and outward displays while under the influence led them to believe she offered herself as a reward for them feeding her desire for more booze. I never asked, but wondered if anyone had stopped to ask why they felt they had a rite of passage to her body. Whatever the case may be, she found a way to survive, as do many others who walk in her shoes. She was not and is not alone in her journey.

Society as a whole has found a way to label people in order to categorize them as being something—an alcoholic, for example—rather than ask the person who or what it is they feel or think they are. Society has also created twelve-step programs to tackle the demon within, and has made it possible for them to stand up and say, "I am an alcoholic," because in part it helps create requests for funding and sustains jobs.

It defines people as being their own worst enemy and affixes labels to them: alcoholic. Drunk. Abuser. Addict. Certain programs do have their merit. However, it begs the question: when will society start allowing people to say, "I use alcohol because I am a survivor. It is my coping mechanism."

This piece is dedicated to the young lady I met that winter's day, wherever she may be, but also to those who find themselves trapped in the same horrors. Not by choice, and certainly not by any personal request. As for my role that day, I merely listened and learned. Despite her own beliefs, alcohol was definitely not her saviour. Nor were her supposed friends.

## Alcohol Saviour

Won't you take a look at me?
Enjoy my perfect outer shell.
Before you discover what's inside,
You'd be better to run like hell.

You enter my life so undoubting,
As I display my pretty face.
Satisfy me with sambuca and beer,
Then conquer my body space.

The mask you find upon my eyes,
Does not cover all of my scars.
For every day that I leave work,
My conscience is attracted to bars.

This poison that I take within,
Is what keeps my inferno alive.
Without my bottle of liquid fuel,
How else would I survive?

To myself this awful addiction,
Will see me through the day.
All I need is one more drink,
Yet I have no credit to pay.

Friends feed my desire for more substances,
Placing myself into an unconscious state.
They take me upstairs to my safe haven,
Without remorse, they begin to violate.

Turning once again to the chalice,
Realizing it's my only true friend.
Now I slip into a downward spiral,
My numb body does descend.

My children, they sleep so peacefully,
For they are unaware of what I do.
Contemplating suicide in drunken stupor,
Three times, I have not followed through.

Although I have told you my secret,
I have considered you my soul mate.
Please move on without me,
Before you find it's too late.

## A New Beginning

FAR TOO OFTEN we are torn apart by others, who exert their beliefs onto us. We become entrapped by their ideologies. It is as if we are unable to think for ourselves, regardless of our own intentions.

A wonderful lady very close to me was a warrior in all she tried and did, and provided me with strength, insight, and guidance every time I went home. She also turned to alcohol to help her get through each day. It seemed to dull all senses and allow her to escape the reality of the shite she was surrounded by and the environment in which she became trapped. The bottles she relied upon never condemned her actions. They did not ask questions, and they were there until the last bittersweet drops applied themselves to her awaiting soul while destroying the human within.

She had been through several unpleasant experiences in life, and regardless of her compassion, bravery, and dedication to family, friends, and complete strangers, and in the face of adversity, she found herself on the outs with everyone. She would not quit due to her personal convictions and remained true to her beliefs in what she fought for right up until her death.

The bottle became her crutch, but the effects of this were not as overpowering as those of her partner, who demanded control within their relationship. She had to seek permission to live her own life, spend money, and go out while trying to live within the sanctity of her home and raising a young family. There was no safety. There was nowhere to go and nowhere to run. She was trapped. The individual she married became the puppet master within their relationship and otherwise controlled her every decision. If she opposed this, she would sadly find herself at the end of his boot or fist, even as she carried their child within her womb (the child that was a product of marital rape).

Statements made during what was ideally supposed to be one of the happiest moments of her life became crippling in their own right. One of the vows exchanged during wedding ceremonies for several years was "to obey and to serve." A social construct created through a patriarchal lens, and in this case it carried tremendous weight in her marriage while shaping what was expected of her and how she was to act.

Many others who have also been faced with the reality of living in a controlled environment end up asking themselves, "What the hell happened?" or "Where did I go wrong?" and may try to seek answers but find themselves stuck. Self-doubts and mind control set in very quickly, and as such the person is not able to fight back from the clutches in which they are now grasped. They become chained to the grind and defined by the rules written within the relationship.

These issues made me question pre-arranged marriages, which do not lessen the impact of what they are: forced. Again, this is constructed through a patriarchal lens where women are seen as less than human, are not allowed to make their own choices, and are bound by the imposed laws set against them. And so their journey begins. Or does it?

We are beginning to see such laws and belief systems being challenged in the fight for human equality by various movements across the world, although this is nowhere near perfect or complete, since these belief systems have been in place since time immemorial. Mulala Yousafzai, a sixteen-year-old student from Pakistan who stood up for her rights as a woman to gain an education, and who survived an assassination attempt by the Taliban, is a prime example.

In my younger days, I noticed priests were only male, while those who cleaned their houses or the church were female. Again, a discrepancy and imbalance in deciding who is seemingly fit to take on assigned roles while creating a further disconnect in what it means to be human.

I constantly heard "Heavenly Father…" being said during mass. This is also depicted in thousands of images of the Holy Spirit. Should I not be able to seek and define that answer for myself? I've since decided that my own spiritual beliefs are something that comes from within me rather than a religious view that was beaten into my very being at school.

As a result of learning her story, I was led to question: since when did humans sign all freedoms of their very beings over to someone else to control through the supposed sanctity of marriage regardless of cultural beliefs or social standing? It made me realize that when one partner is being controlled within a relationship and recognizes that life is no longer in their own hands but is dictated to them by the very person in whom they instilled their trust, love, and respect through the "obey and serve" ideology, the fight for human survival begins.

I believe we have spirit guides that help steer us through the intricacies of life while supporting us in difficult situations. This beautiful warrior shared with me that she reached out for their guidance when the last drops of alcohol were gone and she had no one else to turn to. She ended up turning to her own relatives who had passed away over the years, in the hope that they would give her the courage, belief, and strength she needed to fight another day.

Those days turned to years – over forty of them before she herself passed away a few years ago. The encouragement I learned from her story inspired me to no end when looking at life through her lens and all she'd been through. We all have a cross to bear and a story to tell. But she would no longer let someone else write her story for her, and she took a commanding lead in deciding what that was going to look like, not by someone else's definition.

## A New Beginning

I am a person, and someone I know,
My only true friend is not my foe,
I walk with me in every stride,
My head held high with tremendous pride.

I poured out my soul; I gave all that I had,
In return for my compassion, they said I was mad,
Whether I was awake or as I did sleep,
Into my spirit they drove daggers so deep.

While walking upon me, they poisoned my veins,
They filled me with drink and cast me in chains,
To my own true self, I became such a stranger,
I did not realize that my life was in danger.

The anger inside me has started to burn,
My life is taking a sudden turn,
I'll let this fuel my inner fire,
I'll use the flame to my heart's desire.

This raging inferno that lies so deep within,
Will only be doused with whiskey and gin,
My mind will be dulled and become quite numb,
Allowing others to place me under their thumb.

Others will say my love is so blind,
These others are ignorant, this they will find,
I'll be taken no more as a fool for a wife,
A fresh start I've been granted in this wonderful life.

If my spirit stays strong, I will then see,
I'm the controller of my own destiny,
Those who scratch and claw at my skin,
Will begin to realize that they never shall win.

Although my kinfolk are so far away,
Our hands are entwined with each waking day,
Without ever thinking each time that I breathe,
You walk by my side; you never shall leave.

Your eyes were swollen from the tears you cried,
We saw your inner flame, having almost died,
So be kind to thyself and make a new start,
You have to believe within your own heart.

Creator sits high with pieces from your mold,
Great Spirit did well when creating your soul.
This shaped your being and so we are told,
With principles so high, they can never be sold.

Its time you realized to your own self be true,
Without your strengths, whatever would they do?
These words we share, these words we recite,
Will protect you each morning and comfort you at night.

So before you kneel down ready to pray,
Look in the mirror and to yourself say,
"I'll be filled with such happiness, no room for old strife,
Tomorrow will be the best day of my life."

No longer sigh heavy; no longer despair,
Your heart is now on the road to repair,
Your energy will strengthen and never divide,
Your flame will glow brightly and for others provide.

The courage they need to overcome fright,
To guide them from evil and lead them to light,
To conquer all anguish, to-learn how to laugh,
They will follow so closely, in your chosen path.

If ever you are gripped by an unwelcome fear,
The shadows of darkness will soon disappear,
Our love and kindness will fill you with pride,
New beginnings you'll have, we're here by your side.

# And We Call Ourselves Human?

A FEW YEARS AGO I received an email with an attachment. However, this was not some ordinary photo to look at, laugh, and delete. This picture cast an image in my mind, and one that I have not easily forgotten.

The attachment shows a young child in Sudan being stalked by a vulture merely feet away. Kevin Carter captured this on March 11, 1993, but not long after, he took his own life, seemingly fraught with desperation due to his work as a photographer snapping countless images of children dying from famine. To view this or other photos Kevin took, simply search his name online. Be forewarned though, as the images are both graphic and haunting.

While having a few moments to glance at the television, I watched a program that asked viewers to send money to help children in third world countries attend school. Often, our television screens are filled with requests like this, with Canadian celebrities who have gone overseas on missionary trips to highlight the impoverished conditions faced by the people of these countries.

Personally, I find it overwhelming that we still live in a world where poverty and the right to basic human dignity is seemingly only provided to the world's richest nations. Or is it?

We here in Canada are afforded the luxury of living in a country filled with many natural resources, employment opportunities, and an environment lush with beauty and splendor. However, let us take of our rose-coloured glasses and look a little further outside of the concrete jungles and cities we call home, and to cast our eyes towards communities within a few hours of driving. Right here in our own back garden, we have communities filled with abhorrent living conditions: houses without heat or running water, and where the residents face some of the worst living conditions that people can endure. Reserves.

The impoverishment that one Aboriginal group suffered was captured through the lens of Ila Bussidor and Üstün Bilgen-Reinart through their book *Night Spirit's: The Relocation Story of the Sayisi Dene*. This book depicts some of the horrors and traumas that the Sayisi Dene have faced, including children and families having to feed in rubbish dumps with full-sized bears only feet away from them also scourging for food.

To highlight other discrepancies in 2002, the cost of milk in northern Manitoba First Nations communities was on average $12 for a four-litre jug. Those of us living in urban centres would pay around $3.58 for the exact same product. Fruit and vegetables were often bruised, wilted, or spoiled, so a packet of crisps, a bottle of pop, or a chocolate bar often became the preferred choice among many. It provides a direct understanding of why diabetes is rampant amongst First Nations people.

Print media had featured stories about children on reserve communities across Canada being mauled to death by wild dogs. But these images do not flash across our television screens, nor do we find celebrities from this country bringing heightened awareness to such atrocities. The death of a child, regardless of their location in this world, is a complete and utter tragedy.

No, we do not have projects established to drop bags of rice into these communities, only for mothers to leave their children unattended for a few moments and gather up what they can to feed their families while vultures land behind their children, awaiting famine to provide its next feast. But how is it we have a country plentiful with running water, a resource used to produce hydroelectricity and create outrageous profits for shareholders, but we cannot take some of those profits and create better living conditions in a land that we share with our aboriginal sisters and brothers while ensuring equality for all inhabitants?

Regardless of the luxuries we have or the opportunities we are presented with due to our geographical position, we can no longer ignore conditions that are completely against human dignity right here in Canada and third world countries alike, but also exist throughout this very world. We need to come together collectively, as humans, for humans, and do everything possible to eradicate famine, poverty, and disease, and create a world that provides for each and every one of us regardless of race, culture, or ethnicity. We need the chance to flourish in our little place in space: mother earth. Otherwise, do we have the right to call ourselves human?

# Cry of the Wild

I HAVE OFTEN SAID that there is a parallel between the Indigenous nations and the Irish. Our ancestors lived off the land, had wakes to celebrate the lives of their dead, and spoke traditional languages. They were enslaved by colonizers and forcefully removed from their land. They were left to starve in packs, while Indigenous leaders were forced to sign treaties or have their people starve. For a heartbreaking but insightful read that details much of what happened against four of the Great Chiefs – Poundmaker, Piapot, Crowfoot, and Big Bear – I encourage you to pick up a copy of *Indian Fall: The Last Great Days of the Plains Cree and the Blackfoot Confederacy* by D'Arcy Jenish.

The difference between our cultures and the destruction of our language is that I never received mine until age twelve, while Indigenous people had theirs removed from them at an even earlier age. My language was beaten into me and molested into other students, while it was also sexually violated and beaten out of the Indigenous people through horrific and inhumane actions and deeds after being forcefully sent to attend the Indian Residential School system.

I learned from Elder Raven and many other First Nation friends who are traditional in their worldview how we are related to everything upon this earth. The one-legged, which are the trees. The two-legged, which are our fellow human beings. There are those with wings. And not to forget our four-legged friends, which come in many shapes and sizes. There are those who live and feed in water, which makes up an important part of our very being and our survival.

When I spoke with Elder Raven during my second visit to his community in August 2005, I asked him what form my animal clan was and shared with him that I believed it to be a wolf. He noted that I was not from the wolf clan, but was instead from the beaver clan. I was a little taken aback by this until Elder Raven explained to my oblivious mind that he had watched me work and participate in the teachings that he and his community had to share with my open heart and soul.

My efforts included building tipis, collecting kindling to light the night fire within each tipi, harvesting herbs and berries used to make powerful medicines, gathering and cutting wood that the firekeeper would need for the sweat lodge, and listening and sharing intently with others before helping to make the feast after the sweat or sharing circle ended.

Elder Raven noted that being from the beaver clan means "one who seeks to help all." He went on to say that when a beaver builds a dam, it does not do so for the destruction of the surrounding environment, but to help other animals in the area. As the current from the stream can be incredibly powerful, the beaver builds a dam to slow the flow so that other animals may come by for a drink, stop to eat fish, or cross over to feast on the rich grass on the other side.

As he explained this, a full understanding of who I am and what my journey in life truly meant swept over me. I also received my spirit name that day, which I carry proudly. Sadly, Elder Raven passed away in January 2010. I was granted the beautiful opportunity of eulogizing him at both his wake within the city of Winnipeg at Thunderbird House as well as at his home community. Gitchi Meegwetch, Elder Raven, for welcoming me with an open heart and without passing judgment.

This poem is dedicated to the memory of Elder Garry "Morning Star" Raven. Through his teachings, he provided a gentle guidance to me in my search for knowledge, understanding, and appreciation for the Anishinabe cultural practices and traditional worldviews in Manitoba. I had the immeasurable honour of listening and sharing with Elder Raven in sacred ceremonies, which brought me much healing and spiritual reflection in times of difficulty. Sláinte, mo chara.

## Cry of the Wild

I am of one spirit, placed upon this earth,
My parents were chosen long before my birth.
For now while I grow, I have begun to see,
The animal instinct that lies so deep within me.

The wolf is a creature that is misunderstood,
They say it just hunts for shelter and food.
My own wolf within is my guiding light,
Who protects me from darkness, predators, and fright.

The wolf within teaches me how to survive,
The wolf within uses all senses, there's five.
Touch, taste, smell, hearing, and sight,
The wolf within helps me to fight.

In a world where mankind will steal from his kin,
After the Creator lay down to forgive us from sin.
My wolf from my soul will know not to stray,
My wolf keeps me protected with each brand new day.

You stay by my side with each step that I take,
You protect me forever; your pride you don't fake.
I will listen so intently and hear when you cry,
You'll never abandon me when my time comes to die.

When my sanity is low and I have lost track,
I will call to my wolf, who runs with his pack.
The animal inside me will rear up his head,
Warning those who will harm me, they'd be better off dead.

When I close my eyes and lay me down to sleep,
I have prayed to the Creator for my soul to keep.
Deep inside my flame burns, my wolf he keeps care,
For my spirit, so strong, he keeps from despair.

If you take a good look at yourself inside,
You too shall find an animal with pride.
It might be an eagle, a wolf, a bear, or a deer,
Who will keep you from danger, protect you from fear.

So tomorrow look around you, and you shall soon find,
There has been an animal given to each of mankind.
This animal will guide you to the white pearly gate,
Teach you how to forgive, and lead you from hate.

# Whose "Home and Native Land?"

SINCE EUROPEANS SETTLED on land now called Canada, which is also known in traditional circles as Turtle Island, there has been a huge emphasis to assimilate the aboriginal population into the dominant society. As a student taking my minor degree in Native Studies and while reading through various course materials, including the Report of the Royal Commission on Aboriginal Peoples (RCAP), Volume 1: Looking Forwards, Looking Back, I had learned that in 1920, the Indian Affairs superintendent, Duncan Campbell Scott, stated:

> "I want to get rid of the Indian problem. I do not think as a matter of fact, that the country ought to continuously protect a class of people who are able to stand-alone. Our objective is to continue until there is not a single Indian in Canada that has not been absorbed into the body politic and there is no Indian question, and no Indian department, that is the whole subject of this bill."

Statistics Canada released a survey in 2008 stating that the number of people in Canada who are of aboriginal descent increased significantly to 1,172,790, a rise of 45 percent from 1996. The term "aboriginal" identifies anyone who is First Nations, Inuit, or Métis. This does not account for individuals who had their identity stolen through atrocious tactics of colonization, exploitation, and residential schooling, and do not consider themselves to be of aboriginal ancestry.

Canadian history books, written predominantly to reflect the views of the colonizers, have depicted aboriginal people as savages, beast-like and nomadic and having no sense of guidance or direction.

Many of the traditional values and practices that the aboriginal community held, such as powwows, sundances, and potlatch, were forced into secrecy. Potlatches were sacred ceremonies that marked the birth of a child, a marriage, or the honouring of the deceased. These are spiritual ceremonies that often involved a feast. However, in 1884, the Dominion of Canada saw this custom as a threat and imposed a ban on them. Churches viewed the potlatch as a demonic ritual of Satanism, and were literally hell-bent on Christianizing aboriginals. Those found to be participating in "voodoo" practices were jailed, yet ironically confiscated items from these sacred ceremonies ended up in museums for public display.

Often, being aboriginal has been associated with being shamed. Terms such as "dirty, filthy Indian" were spoken clearly in residential schools. Derogative terminology was the least amount of abuse that the children faced in these torture chambers.

In other countries, residential schools would have been considered internment camps. In Canada, they were viewed as educational settings, removing the "savagery" associated with aboriginal children. However, would someone please enlighten me as to what is educational about whipping repeatedly or beating to death those children who were captured after running away? Or what was educational about scrubbing those children in baths filled with bleach to make their skin appear more white; chopping long braids of hair decorated in beads in no particular fashion or style; slapping children across the face or nailing their tongues to wooden desks for speaking traditional languages; breaking their fingers for writing with their left hand; telling children that traditional cultural ceremonies such as smudging are the devil's work and that those who smudge would burn in hell; having maggots mixed into children's meals; feeding children dog biscuits or, if one was lucky enough, giving them scraps of food leftover from the carefully prepared meals the priests and nuns would consume?

Please explain to me what is educational about a child being raped repeatedly; a child watching nuns birth children borne of young aboriginal boys only to have the newborn placed in a blanket and dropped recklessly upon a fire to dispose of the "sin"; or having young aboriginal females raped by priests only to have their babies confiscated upon their birth, put in shoeboxes, and being left to die while hidden in the school's cold room, or the pregnant females being murdered along with that of their unborn child for threatening to talk?

This information is not recorded in Canadian history books. These truths are told through traditional methods of storytelling. Thousands of aboriginal women and men who survived tactics of colonization and residential schools have shared with unfathomable courage their excruciatingly painful experiences, as it is a part of their healing process in surviving efforts deployed to "remove the Indian problem."

Two such children, who are now adults and continue to live with their unimaginable experiences, shared with immeasurable human courage their unfathomable testimonies of physical, sexual, and emotional abuse in a feature film directed by Tim Wolochatiuk and written by Jason Sherman called "We Were Children." The film is available for purchase through the National Film Board of Canada website.

Duncan Campbell Scott outlined that the purpose of the residential schools was "to kill the Indian within the Indian." Thus why so many First Nations, Inuit, and Métis people do not identify as being aboriginal, and why the census report is vastly under-representative. I have often heard my aboriginal friends describe themselves as being "Red apples," meaning their skin colour is red, but their values and views are white on the inside.

On June 11, 2008, a statement of apology was administered on behalf of Canada by the prime minister in the House of Commons to former students of Indian Residential Schools. The Chair of the Truth and Reconciliation Commission of Canada has gone from coast to coast to coast to capture and document the painful recollections and disclosures of those who suffered abuse within these torture chambers. A feat that simply cannot eradicate years of mental, physical, emotional, spiritual, verbal, and sexual abuse endured by those who faced such atrocious acts of destruction at the hands of another human. A feat that cannot bring back lives of those whose died at the hands of their abusers.

There is a traditional saying amongst the Indigenous population: "For as long as the sun shines, the grass grows, and the waters flow." We also have a saying back home in Ireland: "Only our rivers run free." I can only hope that somehow and through much holistic healing, our sisters and brothers who have had their identities stolen are proud to be counted as aboriginal peoples and fully reflect in freedom: the large population of First Nations, Inuit, and Métis people who live on this, their "home and native land" called Turtle Island.

My hopes are that those who now live with the intergenerational effects and blood memories as a result of the Indian Residential Schools are supported to find healing, whether through western methods of counseling or traditional methods of sharing and healing circles.

Both the North and South of Ireland could fully benefit from that healing as well, since Boarding Schools and those run by Christian brothers hold similar dark secrets as locked within their walls made of brick, mortar, and plaster.

## Hearts Entwined

I AM OFTEN AMAZED at those couples whose relationships have lasted forty, fifty, and even sixty-plus years. It certainly is a testimony to the vow they gave to one another on their wedding day, and to having spent their entire lives together, no matter the changes the world has gone through. There have also been documented cases where one partner passed away only to be followed into the grave within a few months by the other partner, as they could not seem to cope or live without their soul mate. As one journey ends, a new celebration is just beginning.

Many have found their life partner. When the time is right, they begin planning for the special day – a union of two hearts. The cost nowadays however seems to have become more of an important factor than the actual day itself. The stress of planning the wedding can almost become the collapse of it, as everyone wants to add his or her input.

Although friends and family may give advice to try and help guide their journey in life, it comes down to the couple to seek that happiness together and work their way through what lies ahead. After all, two different people who have found similar interests and want to spend the rest of their lives together have to bring a balance of equality into the marriage. Regardless of the pressures that life has to offer, finding the time to spend with one another should remain a priority. Being human is to be imperfect, and marriage, just like any other relationship, goes through the ebb and flow of highs and lows.

To those who have come to, crossed, and remain within this arrangement, and for those of you who are only in the beginning stages of this part of your life, this poem is for you. Listen to your partner with open ears long after the wedding vows have been exchanged, the magic of the day has passed, and you both continue to persevere through life's little challenges. No one ever said it was or will be easy. Reaching that golden anniversary takes a lot of work.

### Hearts Entwined

Our families are gathered, and many a friend,
To witness this blessing, they do descend.
The music begins to our guests' delight,
"Here comes the bride all dressed in white."

We stand at this altar; we desire no fear,
This day we have waited so long to near.
Our will to succeed with the future untold,
We will always feel comfort and never be cold.

Although our days have their ups and downs,
Our smiling lips, they sometimes show frowns.
This adventure we'll challenge as husband and wife,
Stick together we shall through this journey called life.

This day together we are united as one,
To complete our world, never becoming undone.
My heart you are, and forever you'll be,
I am your soul, this you will see.

Take my hand and the rest of me,
Into your life, I forever shall be.
Our hearts combined will beat as one drum,
Will only seek fulfillment and never feel numb.

Our hands are joined in holy matrimony,
Our love is divine, never proving phony.
'Til death do us part is the vow that we keep,
Through the shadows of darkness we never shall sleep.

Every new morning that will look upon us,
Will see us make happiness even when we fuss.
Our moments of sadness will soon fade away,
So long as we are together at the end of each day.

This is our moment, which we celebrate,
Reaching destiny, we've discovered our fate.
In the stars beyond and when we do meet,
Our hearts entwined will continue to beat.

## Little Angel

ROBERT MUNCH WROTE *Love You Forever*, a children's book that parents have passed on from family member to friend, mother to son, and father to daughter with the birth of a new child. This book is a treasured classic. It is one I read many times to my own two children, and it is hard to read without getting teary eyed due to the love expressed in it from a mother to her baby son, and then from her son, who becomes a father himself but has to nurse his mum as well as his own baby daughter.

Being a dad is no easy feat. It takes a great amount of dedication and responsibility to step up to the plate when bringing a child into the world. It takes someone with determination to face the unknown. In being a first-time father, having never held a baby in their arms before and with no instruction manual to guide one through the multitude of steps that it takes to raise a child, one has to learn what they were taught from their parents.

Unfortunately, not every child is granted that opportunity, as their parents may be following or repeating cycles that were introduced to them as children such as violence or other forms of abuse. Others may not know how to express love, comfort, compassion, hugs, or kisses. Sadly, I have seen this by those who remain directly impacted by the intergenerational effects of Indian Residential Schools. Their parents lost the ability to express human emotion and feeling due to their experiences. One colleague shared that during a workshop she held and when asking what they would like for Christmas, one of the children said, "I just want my mum and dad to tell me that they love me. I'm fourteen-years-old and I have never experienced what that is like."

Along with the birth comes the responsibility of trying to be a good partner or husband. Often, children in their innocence become the wedge between two parents who are arguing, stepping in and asking them to stop fighting. Others hide behind furniture, lock themselves in a bedroom, or exhibit other signs of trauma including bedwetting. The child ends up getting punished for this behaviour, although they are simply reacting to the negative impacts of their surrounding environment. Not every child can express what they are feeling, or internalize the divide between their parents as being their fault. But with the collapse of so many relationships these days, children often get stuck in the middle of two parents fighting for custody, or one parent walking away and leaving the other parent to fend for themselves and without financial support to help raise the children. The impacts can be long-lasting in the developing mind of a child. They should not be used as pawns in any relationship, for they were not brought into this world for that purpose, nor should their precious little minds be poisoned with venomous hatred by one parent against the other.

I have known many dads who have faced this reality. To further clarify, I am speaking to those dads who play an important role in their children's lives. Anyone can be a father, but not everyone can be a dad. The struggles faced in difficult relationships where resolution could not be reached, and the uncertainty of what their child may go through can cause strain. One must consider what affects the child and the dad will experience in not seeing each other every day.

I have often said that we should look at the world through the innocent eyes of a child before having that shattered by the biases and environments in which they are raised. Certain segments within Northern Ireland are perfect examples of that. As adults, we have our worldviews defined, but we should not place our bitterness onto the loving, open hearts, and learning minds of innocent children.

One of the traditional teachings shared by Elder Raven is that it is our role to prepare for the next seven generations. With that said, if parents can put their differences aside and work together in the best interests of their children, this would create a society that would benefit the world over. The same is said for living together in harmony and not living in the past. Give peace a chance. Love your kids unconditionally.

## Little Angel

I know a young lad from a local town,
In these last few years, he has done nothing but frown.
His life, it has changed from bad to worse,
It seems unto him there has been placed a curse.

He married a girl, he was happy and all,
In the first few years they had such a ball.
Now as he reflects on the years gone by,
There is only one person for whom he would die.

Her name is important; his daughter is she,
She filled up his life with musical harmony.
He is so scared to let her go,
Without her around, his life will be low.

The years have passed since she was born,
And now from her, his life will be torn.
He will no longer see her face everyday,
She's his pride and joy; she wants him to stay.

But how can he stay in a marriage of no love?
With his little one sacred, as peaceful as a dove.
He can draw her a picture or put lines in the sand,
Of her mummy and daddy, divided they stand.

Into her wee heart will be nothing but pain,
Because her wee world is no longer the same.
How can she be shown what's wrong from right,
When all she sees is her parents fight.

She does not deserve this ritual of sin,
Because in the end, neither one of them will win.
His daughter is so innocent, so precious, so pure,
These ugly onslaughts she needn't endure.

Each breath he inhales, every step that he takes,
Each beat from his heart, every morning he wakes,
He thinks of his daughter with happiness in mind,
How could he ever leave his child behind?

He was the first to hold her within human arms,
Immediately she started to show all her charms.
His little precious angel, he wants you to know,
Your daddy will love you, no matter where he will go.

It is so wrong for your parents to fight,
From early in the morning to the late hours of night.
He knows you can't understand the battles and fuss,
The emotions they portray, the words that they cuss.

And in between them, you make your wee stand,
You try your very best to lend a wee hand.
To correct the problem and become the glue,
Of your mother and father, divided in two.

They have both grown to love you so very, very much,
But now with each other, they have become out of touch.
Their love for you will always remain strong,
Please understand that you have done nothing wrong.

Life is a journey; we follow a path,
Sometimes we cry, sometimes we laugh.
While he sits here now and writes out this poem,
His heart, it is heavy, for you both face the unknown.

Will he get to see your smiling face every day?
Hear the words you recite, watch the fun as you play?
Clean your hands and face after you've eaten so well?
Kiss and tuck you in goodnight with a hug that is swell?

This is the future; he may face it alone,
If he's not with you daily, he'll rely on the phone,
To keep him in touch with his baby so dear,
And right by your side, he will always be near.

You are his own gift, for which he is glad,
You are his wee miracle, and he is your dad.
Never will he feel love again so deep,
That he does with his daughter, who makes his heart leap.

Keep humming the songs you've known for awhile,
For whenever you sing, it makes him smile.
If you ever feel sad, please don't despair,
His baby you are, Daddy will always be there.

# Lament for a Child

A BEAUTIFUL FRIEND BECAME a special part of my degree throughout four years of study together. We were both parents, returning to university after spending many years in the workforce, and we recognized the potential a degree would afford us based on our life experience. We would speak in volumes about our children. Their quirks, and how funny they were in teaching us about the world around them, but as seen and defined through their eyes.

We graduated separately and wished each other a successful future with our newfound career paths. However, a few years later, a tragic event made time stand still. I was working, and while speaking to a co-worker, my mobile phone buzzed on my hip. I picked up the phone only to read a text from a colleague I also attended university with. It said that my friend's child had been taken from us. My breath escaped from me with a sudden gasp. My mind went into overdrive, trying to figure out what had happened but I would have to wait several grueling days to learn that answer. All I knew was that the Creator needed an angel.

I attended the funeral, which was heartbreaking. As any parent can attest, a child can obviously touch the lives of everyone who has had the pleasure of meeting or knowing them. We spend every waking minute worrying about their wellbeing, making sure they are fed, clothed, and take care of their every need such as cleaning scraped knees, applying ice to bruises, kissing their owee's better, and giving them a warm hug before tucking them in at bedtime. We play roles as Santa, the Tooth Fairy, and the Easter Bunny for our children.

Upon returning from the internment, I wanted to cry hard for my dear friend. Lost in thought, I made my way home but could not seem to shake the words that were floating through my head. I set about to write them down.

## Lament for a Child

The day started out with heartache,
Knowing what we had to do.
Make our way to the service,
And bid a fond farewell to you.

Your pictures up upon the screen,
Countless tears did fall.
The lives and hearts your love has filled,
Echoed through the hall.

No one could have prepared us,
In our time to say goodbye.
Creator called you to heaven,
Sweet angel in the sky.

We saw the signs you sent today,
And counted them: one, two, three.
You wanted to show everyone,
"Hey look, I am still among thee."

The dragonfly within the crowd,
It touched each one of us.
"It's me, your little angel,
So please don't make a fuss.

I fly so free amongst you all,
Look up into the sky.
I'm one of the birds you now see,
It's not time to say goodbye.

The warmth you feel upon your face,
As provided by the sun.
Shhh… it's really me sending my love,
To each and every one.

I'll see you someday in heaven,
And will come to play with you.
That blinking star in the sky,
It's me winking back at you.

Although our time was short,
And now we have to part.
I will always be your precious child,
I'll live on within your heart."

One of the most peaceful outcomes of this—if that can be said about the passing of a child—is the gift of teaching in death. There were so many signs that life does indeed continue after we have been called upon from this journey on earth. Guidance only an angel can provide.

The day following the service I went back to the cemetery to read this lament in private. I could not find the graveyard for the life of me. I drove down many gravel roads, into a farmer's field, and even asked at the local store where the graveyard was, but no one had ever heard of it. I was on the verge of giving up and saying that I was sorry that I could not find the final resting place. Determined, I figured I would go back to the main highway and try one last time.

Driving along, with no sense of direction and no one around me, suddenly in my rear view mirror I could see a vehicle in the distance. Figuring I would turn left at the next gravel road, I drove on a bit further. Even though I had left my turn signal on, I decided to pull off to the right instead. The next thing I knew, the vehicle that had been following me made a left turn down the gravel road that lay directly across from me.

I thought I could maybe follow and ask for directions when the driver pulled over. As I learned the day before, the loose gravel kicked up by a procession of vehicles creates a mini dust storm, but regardless of this, I could see the vehicles both ahead of and behind me. However, on this day, although I could still see in front of me, I could not see the vehicle itself. Just dust. There was nothing behind me.

Suddenly the dust lifted, but the vehicle was gone! It had come from out of nowhere and disappeared without explanation. I looked in every direction for it, but it had nowhere to go and no other dust trail could be seen. The next thing that happened left me in awe, shock, and amazement. The cemetery was on my right-hand side. I almost passed it while trying to look for the vehicle and its driver. I guess I had been provided with the guidance I'd silently asked for.

Needless to say I was freaked out from this experience, for there was absolutely no reason for what had just happened other than it was a sign. I entered the graveyard at a gentle pace and decided to read a copy of the lament, but as I did I noticed that the sun was not beating down from the sky this time but was shining on me from behind a tree. It seemed to be playing a game of hide and seek.

A dragonfly came buzzing around me, which made me laugh at the innocence of a child telling me that I was not to worry.

When I reached the part about the birds, unlike the previous day, I looked up towards the sky, but there was nothing overhead to be seen. Before I could blink, out of the corner of the cemetery three birds a lot smaller than the huge ones I had seen the day before came out from the grass behind me, flew the length of the graveyard, and then parted ways while flying out towards the sun. Each of the signs I had captured within the lament occurred all over again!

The grave was beautifully decorated. An angel, whose precious love and memory continues to live on within the hearts and minds of those who had the pleasure of being a part of this child's life. Rest in peace, little one. Thank you for the blessings you provided and for reminding us that life does indeed go on after death.

## Empty Promises

W HILE WATCHING TV one day, I was blown away by celebrity marriages, some of which are borne completely for selfish reasons. Players on the Hollywood scene seemingly have their own definition of what is socially acceptable. They set themselves apart through standards of high society. One extravagant, ridiculously expensive wedding that cost tens of millions of dollars lasted less than six months. Although we commonly see this in the tabloid newspapers, does their celebrity status set them apart and make them holier than thou? Imagine what we could do with that money: providing antiretroviral medications to those who cannot afford this forty-cents per day, lifesaving drug in some of the poorest nations of the world where HIV is rampant and most prevalent.

Take another marriage that made headline news: a young buxom woman marrying a man well into his golden years. This becomes acceptable in the minds of some, as the man made his fortunes and can "pick and choose" who he wants to be with. After he died, the woman was viewed as being immoral, greedy, and looking for a "sugar daddy." Sickeningly though, when these roles are reversed and an older woman sets eyes upon a younger man, she is called a "cougar." Who decides what is right from wrong between each type of engagement between two people of legal age, whether it be an older woman choosing a younger man or vice versa? Why does society get to define and apply these terms? Is it simply easier to pass judgment than to try and understand? Is their happiness in becoming a couple open to judgment through another's lens? Or does the almighty dollar define the sanctity of what marriage in Hollywood is all about: flash, pizzazz, paparazzi, pompous behaviour, and elite social class and standing, or who can sell the most tabloid magazines?

While this is going on, we find ourselves engrossed with the latest buzz, and become glossy eyed over the latest fashion faux pas or other star-studded, red carpet appearances. We turn to Twitter to share one hundred and forty characters in making the latest gossip trend as to who is sleeping with who, yet thousands are starving and subsequently dying from poverty, famine, and diseases that are easily treated without first lining the pocket of a CEO of a major pharmaceutical corporation. Almost a script directly out of a Hollywood production, but this in fact is a real-life daily occurrence.

Some cultures afford men the right to choose their bride regardless of age. In other religious sects, one man is granted the opportunity to marry a number of women past his first marriage. It begs the question: does the sanctity of marriage not apply in these circles?

## Empty Promises

On our day of wedding bliss,
These promises I presented to you.
Though now I reflect on the promises we made,
All but one has fallen through.

You promised me you would never leave,
We would only part in death.
All of your promises were sacred words,
While mine were a waste of breath.

I promised you we two were one,
That there would be no other.
But while I gazed into your eyes,
I thought of yet another.

I promised you I would always be there,
Nothing would keep us apart.
Though every day we were together,
'Twas no room for you in my heart.

I promised you when I became angry or mad,
My thoughts would extinguish the fuse.
Although I would not physically assault,
My words would continue the abuse.

I promised I would take care of you,
In sickness and in health.
I promised these words only because,
Your insurance would secure my wealth.

I promised that I would weep for you,
When your time did come to die.
No matter how hard I would force myself,
There were no tears to cry.

The parting words you did fulfill,
With that we were given no choice.
Now that you are finally at peace,
Nevermore will I promise by voice.

# Bruised and Battered

A FTER MOVING TO Canada, and in speaking with several girls at school who became good friends after getting over their not so secret crush on my accent, I could never really comprehend why they stayed with their abusive boyfriends. The story had a consistent theme: he got drunk or high, and would then abuse her verbally by calling her demeaning names. She was abused mentally in that he would ask her repeated questions but slightly changed them each time to try and get her to say what he wanted to hear her say, not the truth she was already speaking.

Antagonist practices of emotional abuse were then utilized by telling her that she was not good enough, and that if he left no man would ever want to be with her as she was already "well used" and no one would want "leftovers" or "sloppy seconds."

Other forms of abuse were spiritual in nature, which ripped out the very soul of the young lady while making her feel worthless in every which way, only allowing her to have happiness as seen through his eyes. If he was happy, then what was she complaining about?

Last was the physical abuse that came in a variety of degrading forms, including sexual.

When disclosing details of their relationship or seeking advice, I would often ask why friends chose to stay with their boyfriends, who caused so much pain and grief and would remain on the receiving end of such abusive behaviour. What struck me is that the answer would always be the same: "I love him." My response was almost scripted too: "When you love someone, you do not treat him or her like they are nothing to you, no matter who is giving the abuse and who is on the receiving end of it." Regardless of the advice given, my friends who had the courage to share often went back after an apology was received from their abuser, only for the cycle to start all over again the following week.

While in university, I took a family violence course in human ecology. I argued with one of my professors why the term rape is now referred to as sexual abuse? Rape is rape, no matter how one tries to define it. This is an act that is a complete victimization, degradation, and demoralization of a person along with their body, mind, and soul. I struggled with this issue. Due to the politically sensitive world we now find ourselves living in, we have begun desensitizing such an incredibly destructive action by adding an all-encompassing label.

As I have seen, there are many women who abide by traditional perspectives and follow a patriarchally defined lifestyle that may not be by choice or want. The same principle applies to those who find themselves in abusive relationships and seemingly have reasons to excuse their partner's actions.

"I upset him, thus the reason he became angry."

"If I just cooked his meal the way he likes it, he would never have called me those names."

"If I could only do more to make him happy, maybe he would love me the way that I know he does."

These are not excuses, but are mindsets that become almost permanent in nature for someone who has been repeatedly abused over the years and may not realize she has been programmed to respond in one-manner or face consequences. Sadly, and as miserable as it may be, there are those who feel this is their calling in life and can do nothing about it.

It boils down to the cycle of violence theory that can be found in any human ecology course or textbook. However, those holding the power in any relationship are nothing without their partner, who unwittingly or perhaps unknowingly maintains a perfect imbalance. To top that, where would any of us be without the nurturing love and care that a woman provides in bringing us to life? Without women, our lives are not possible. With today's technology and if women so choose, life could continue through the donation and preservation of sperm. The course of history could certainly be very different.

Unfortunately, I have friends who are in this exact predicament and have literally suffered in complete silence for years from the abuses they continue to undergo. They, along with others I do not know, feel that they have made their decision and are to live and die by them. They are terrified to leave their abusers, and in having suffered so many years of psychological trauma, feel completely worthless and undeserving of a better life and remain in a negative environment.

I have one friend who has been molded to follow a regimented routine. She panics constantly in case she were to forget one of her assigned actions. She has been called some of the most degrading and humiliating names that a woman could ever endure, even after bearing two children who she has raised alone for her partner. She is not allowed to answer the phone or have any friends. She is not allowed to have a drivers licence, and is brought to work and picked up again to make sure she comes home to take care of the house and all else assigned to her. When she cries or falls to pieces from what her life has become and how she has been treated, she is degraded that much further. If another man looks in her direction, she is punished when she gets home and reminded that only "he" has the right to look at her, even though she never acknowledged the gesture to begin with.

I would like to dedicate this composition to my dear friend, who unfortunately after twenty years of being trapped in her own hell, continues to suffer in complete silence, but also to all women who have gone through years of abuse in past or current relationships. I dedicate in the hope that this brings some form of light to their stories, no matter how small, and all they have gone through so that others may look for the signs of abuse and hopefully find help for them before they become fully disconnected from the support networks that are available.

As I have said, we all have a cross to bear and a unique story to tell. This is her story.

## Bruised And Battered

*Welcoming him home from work,*
*She promised his favourite meal.*
*Offered a kiss before she cooked,*
*A dish of breaded veal.*

It wasn't what he wanted,
Telling her to get out of his face.
He'd already had a rough day,
Plenty more work yet to chase.

*She stated her apology,*
*And offered to make things right.*
*Sweetly she asked, "Will you join me,*
*In a bubble bath tonight?"*

His response, as sharp as daggers,
"I've so much more to do!
Countless deadlines to meet,
Wasted dollars supporting you."

*"Baby, you know I miss you," she sobbed,*
*"We never share quality time.*
*Is loving you deeply as I do,*
*Such a terrible crime?"*

"What's wrong with you?" he screamed,
"Will you quit annoying me?
Once again you're under my skin,
Making me so very angry!"

*"But honey, I love you so much!" she did cry,*
*"When not with you, I'm sad.*
*I only wanted to ensure your happiness,*
*I didn't mean to make you mad."*

His rising hand, it slapped her face,
She fell like a lump of lard.
"Oh baby, can't you see I'm sorry,
I didn't mean to hit you so hard."

*Her crumpled body upon the floor,*
*Her rosy cheek did sting.*
*Her trembling hand covering the bruise,*
*Left there by his high school ring.*

Kneeling down onto the floor,
As he looked her in the eye.
"Baby, I really didn't mean it this time,"
One hand upon his fly.

*She knew his sorrow meant nothing,*
*As her head began to throb.*
*He grabbed a handful of golden hair,*
*Her mouth began to bob.*

"Baby, you know I really do love you,
When you take good care of me."
He would not let go of his grasp,
Until she had finished he.

*Paralyzed by all her fear,*
*She asked, "Baby, did that feel good?"*
*Hoping just as she always did,*
*Her deed would lighten the mood.*

"That makes things so much better,
Let's continue on with our day.
Good thing you know what best for you,"
He muttered while walking away.

*As she rose up from the floor,*
*She prayed that it would end.*
*"Some day when I will find the strength,*
*My broken heart will mend."*

Sitting back down at his desk,
His actions now in the past.
"Hey, when am I getting my dinner?
You'd better make it real fast."

*She went to fix his plate,*
*And brought to him his meal.*
"How did you know what I wanted?" he asked,
Upon seeing the breaded veal.

Many years have since passed,
Her heart remains broken and shattered.
Her pain hidden behind a fractured smile,
Her face still bruised and battered.

## Hate Crimes Against Humanity

REGARDLESS OF COUNTLESS movements to create awareness and acceptance of people who identify their sexual orientation with the lesbian, gay, bi-sexual, transgendered, and two-spirited community (or LGBTT for short), and with issues surrounding the host nation of the 2014 Sochi Winter Olympics targeting this marginalized population, it identifies how massive of a problem society continues to create for certain groups through unprecedented hate crimes.

While attending university, I had heard a story of a child who was gunned down for being openly gay. His name was Lawrence King. He was fifteen years of age and in the eighth grade.

In the reports that emerged from the killing of this child, students were quoted as saying that King freaked the males out because he wore make-up, jewelry, painted his nails, and dressed in clothing deemed to be for the opposite sex. Since when does that provide an open ticket for another student to take the life of a person for his or her style of clothing, appearance, or sexual orientation? And sadly, not only did one set of parents lose their child that day, the parents of the fourteen-year-old who took King's life was charged with second degree murder and is currently serving a sentence upwards of twenty-five years in a US federal prison.

It is not just those from the LGBTT community that find themselves pushed to the fringes of society. Children who have been born with both sets of genitalia are called hermaphrodites, yet are often seen as being anomalies. There are documented cases of parents who are mortified to learn of this "birth accident," and have decided to raise their child as one gender, making the decision to perform surgical reassignment surgery to "correct this" only to learn that as their child grows, she or he identifies as being the gender opposite to that chosen for them.

As taught in my feminist perspectives class, sexuality is not static but fluid. It has been researched and documented that many people who identify as heterosexual may become curious about having a same-sex partner, even if only on one occasion. But they do not deem themselves as being gay or a lesbian. They do not stress about using the socialized term of "coming out of the closet" or worry about facing discrimination, being rejected, or being fired from their jobs for their disclosure. Or, in the case of Lawrence King, being murdered.

The time has come when we need to stop targeting people as being different from us due to their sexual orientation. The time has come for us to realize that gender is not a dyad as has been socially constructed, but that a person who is borne of both sets of genitals makes gender a triad. The time has come for us to put an end to hate crimes, to break down barriers and stop the taunting, labeling, and segregation of people due to their choice of lifestyle. Now is the time to come together as a collective, appreciate our differences and uniqueness as individuals, and work together under the construction of one race: the human race.

## Disposable Humans

IN CANADA THERE is a stretch of highway that has been renamed by some as the Highway of Tears. Countless missing and murdered women, who unfortunately were involved in the sex trade, have met an untimely demise while travelling along this highway. The majority of them are also aboriginal. Numerous families continue to fight for justice and in hopefully finding their missing loved ones. But why is it that a woman who regrettably finds herself caught up in this industry is seen as less than human, defined as a slut, a whore, a skank, and a piece of meat, among other forms of degrading terminology? Why is it that this is considered acceptable by today's standards? Is it because of their background that this is often overlooked?

The sex trade is one of the world's oldest professions. Many will refer to those involved in this seedy industry as prostitutes or hookers. I find these terms degrading, as several women who are trapped within this dark line of work are not there by personal choice.

In major cities across the world, there are thousands of single mums who have escaped abusive relationships and are reliant on social welfare to try and raise their family while often going without a meal themselves. Due to lucrative monies that can be made within the sex trade, several have turned to this industry in order to provide and make ends meet for their families. However, to cope with selling their bodies each night to different strangers, narcotics are used to numb the pain. What is just as degrading though are those who neglect to see the human on the street and throw objects such as pennies at them.

As a student, I learned of a high-profile individual in one Canadian city who would buy oral pleasures from sex trade workers. Fifteen dollars was merely pocket change to the judge, but to the women fulfilling his request, they could buy another substance hit to fill their veins. Within two weeks though, the judge would often see these same women in his courtroom and blast them as being a disgrace to society, as being nothing more than dirt and filth and lucky he did not throw the book at them. Did these thoughts cross his mind upon reaching orgasm?

How is it that a society which deems itself progressive in ensuring that women receive equal status and stature can ignore this and allow for such traumas and abuses to occur? Furthermore, why is it that the women involved with this practice are busted time and time again by law enforcement officials, yet the men who purchase such services from these women get lighter sentences and are not faced with the same stigmas as the sex trade workers? Are they defined by society as beings that are less than human who should be punished for their crimes?

What is often neglected when soliciting a sex trade worker is that every one of these women who has undergone these sorts of traumas to her body began life in a sacred place: the womb. These women are someone's child. They are someone's daughter. They are someone's friend, and in many cases, they are also someone's mother. However, these values are often misplaced, neglected, or not even considered when sexual gratification through power and control is the only thing that is sought.

This piece is fully dedicated to those women who have found themselves trapped within the sex trade and are often ostracized by society for who they have become in trying to survive. This piece is further dedicated to the countless missing and murdered women not only in Canada, but also around the world, who have met an untimely fate at the hands of those who solicited them in the first place. My hope is that this increases awareness to those of us who fortunately are not on the streets tonight, trying to survive.

## Disposable Human

A broken life, a broken home,
Out on the streets I dwell.
In order to survive each night alone,
My body I hate to sell.

But living out here, I have no choice,
To keep myself alive.
Crack, cocaine, and heroin,
My friends help me survive.

Strangers lurk within the dark,
Begging service for a fee.
Roughly, they enter my body,
No love for whom they see.

For all I am is disposable,
In the minds of those I please.
They do not see me as human,
Nothing more than just a sleaze.

So do not look into my eyes,
Or question for my name.
Dump yourself inside my soul,
And leave me with your shame.

You really are no different,
From each trick I've met before.
Take me, pay me, use me,
And kick me out the door.

I'll pick up all the pieces,
Once you've done your filthy deed.
Now awaiting my next customer,
To fulfill their sexual need.

This cycle will repeat itself,
All throughout the night.
Dirty money within my hand,
Will soon be gone from sight.

Although my life is broken,
My home was filled with pain.
Please note I'm someone's daughter,
Before you seek me out again.

## Surreal, Nine One One

I'VE HEARD MANY people recollect where they were on the day when John F. Kennedy, the thirty-fifth President of the United States of America, was shot dead in 1963. Others may choose to remember when it was announced that Elvis Presley had died in 1977. There are those who recall when John Lennon was killed outside his New York apartment in 1980. Honestly, I never knew any of these events, as John F. Kennedy was killed seven years before I was born. Elvis died seven years after. I did not know who the Beatles were until much later in life.

On September 11, 2001, however, I know exactly where I was, what I was doing, and the impacts that day had on me. I was working for a cable company and had to pick up my colleague Tim from his apartment as I did each day before setting out to our worksite. It was 7:54 in the morning, and I was listening to a local radio station. The DJ came on with a breaking news announcement: it appeared that a plane had flown into the World Trade Center.

I whipped out my cell phone and called Tim, asking him to put on CNN and tell me what he was seeing. He was not sure what I was on about, so I explained what I had just heard on the radio. Sure enough, he confirmed that the World Trade Center had massive amounts of smoke billowing out from it. Shortly thereafter I reached the parking lot of his apartment building and scrambled up to his floor to see the devastating images for myself.

The horror of seeing people leaping from the burning building and hearing the crashes above the firemen on-site from the bodies making their impact was deafening. I sat glued to the TV screen while Tim popped his head in and out of his kitchen to catch a glimpse of the destruction occurring in New York City. I couldn't move, and like millions of other people, I sat in absolute horror at the images flashing across the screen.

I screamed, "Tim, there's a second plane, there's another plane!" accompanied by a bunch of expletives when the South Tower was hit, leaving a devastating hole in the side of that building. The images that followed included the towers burning and people running, screaming, and dying. It was complete chaos compared to the everyday work scenes that would have normally played out in the streets of New York.

My boss had phoned during this time to find out were Tim and I where and came to his apartment. He didn't seem fazed by the events that were unfolding and wanted us to get out and get the day started. I guess the almighty dollar was more important to him than the lives of thousands of people who were affected by this. We left and headed for work.

As time ticked along, news also broke that the Pentagon had been attacked and that another plane had been hijacked. Knowing my brother Joe was in Hawaii and that there was a large military base located near Pearl Harbor, I began frantically phoning him to get his TV switched on immediately. It was after 3am there, but he never did pick up. I left him a few panicked messages from my company cell phone, telling him to get out of his location and to watch for incoming planes. Shortly thereafter all phone lines into America went dead.

The psychosocial impacts of September 11, 2001 were felt far and wide across this world, and there is still tremendous fallout from this event twelve years later. This poem is dedicated to the memory of those who lost their lives on this dreadful day, which we now memorialize through yearly reflection, and to the men and women who responded to this event and to those whose lives were forever changed.

### Surreal, Nine One One

While I sit, my eyes are glued to TV,
Horrifying images reflect back at me.
Unable to move, I'm in disbelief,
America attacked; the whole world is in grief.

Innocent people from all walks of life,
Tried to give help to comrades in strife.
Lifeless beings now trapped in a cell,
The World Trade Center has turned into hell.

These scenes I view, could this be a dream?
Deep down inside I just want to scream.
It seems so surreal, like a deadly nightmare,
I open my eyes and continue to stare.

Brave men and women, their hands they lent,
To rescue others was their intent.
A courageous search on a crumpled floor,
The towers collapse, their lives no more.

I watch so many, they shout and cry,
Thousands did not deserve to die.
While I stare at my screen, I kneel and pray,
For America to see light at the end of the day.

Although right now the world feels numb,
Those responsible, they have not won.
We are a nation and we stand free,
God Bless America, please God, bless me.

## Going Forward in Reverse

WE ARE OFTEN asked, "Did you get out of the wrong side of the bed this morning?" This may be reflective of a mood, or just that nothing has gone right. Clothes freshly washed and pressed for a corporate presentation fell on the floor during the night, and you have no time to sort them again. The hot water tank has blown, and the day starts off with a cold shower. The alarm clock was set for an early morning interview, only to see that there was a power outage. After filling the dog's bowl with fresh water, dry kibble is absentmindedly put into the same dish. Such events put the day into disarray, and only seem to compound as time goes on. Everything is backwards. It is almost as if someone flipped our left and right brain while we slept. During events such as these, we might just find ourselves wishing for the day to be over, yet it has only just begun.

There are also times in the middle of the day when work seems to present an overload, leading to brain drain, and nothing else makes any sense whatsoever no matter how hard we try. Some of us may find ourselves laughing as a coping mechanism while asking what else could possibly go wrong. There are those days that no matter what we try to do, regardless of how many times we have done it before seamlessly, it is just not going to work. Or in the evening while taking an unexpected but light nap, only to wake up and leap out of the chair in a complete panic, thinking we have overslept and have to get to work. We frantically rush around, only to then realize that it is still the same day.

Life is all about reflections from special moments created. Friends from my high school days have gone back through yearbook photos and, upon looking at the hairdo that was backcombed and sits at least a foot off their heads with all sorts of hairspray, now say it was one of the most embarrassing things they could have ever done. A moment in life which they believed was completely perfect in that they looked their best and thought they were to cool for school, only to look back years later and ask, "What in the world was I thinking?"

We have all gone through such incidents and really cannot turn back time to reverse what we thought was magical at that moment. We have to embrace those moments for whatever they were at the time. It's part of being human and living life.

## Going Forward in Reverse

What would you do?
In the middle of the night,
If the moon was dark blue,
And the sky was brilliant white.

Would you fall down to your knees,
Each time someone said please?
Allow them access to your banks,
Every time they said thanks.

When times are extremely hard,
Nothing at all seems funny.
Would you use your credit card,
And spend that plastic money?

Would you try to twiddle your thumb?
Though it's extraordinarily numb.
From that sharp and pointy hook,
Found in a professional fishing book.

Although you're trapped in hell,
When you kneel down ready to pray.
Would you say that you're quite well?
To the man of disarray.

Would you try to write a letter?
Though your printing is no better.
Than when you were in school,
You thought you were so cool.

If your car went on red,
And would not go on green.
Would you stay in bed?
For it caused you quite the scene.

Although you run lightning fast,
Would you take the gum from your shoe?
You finished the race dead last,
Because it stuck to you like glue.

If this is your reflection right now,
It's time to take a bow.
'Cause this is my final verse,
Of you going forward in reverse.

# A Time to Reflect

IN 2010, WHEN I was home for Rosie's wedding, I sat with Denis in his parent's house. He himself is now a father with young children. Just like our family did in 1985, he has also since left and gone on to pursue a career path elsewhere in the world.

As we chatted over a cup of coffee, I told him that I had often wondered about the direction in which life had taken him and spoke about my writing of the poem "Scattered Youth." I told Denis that I had yearned to come back to all of my mates for what I thought I was missing out on, and how my homesickness had controlled my thoughts for eighteen years.

Without blinking an eye, he set my mind straight. Denis turned to me and said, "Why would you mourn for this hole? When you left in 1985, all of us were like 'Greg is such a jammie bastard getting to move to Canada. We wish we could move away from this place too.'" He hit me with an answer I would never have expected from him.

He continued his thoughts. "After you were gone, we were constantly getting beaten up by gangs in the Doagh Road forest. There was nothing here for any of us. You were lucky to get away when you did. If you think back, how many of us have also done the same and moved away for better opportunity? Believe me, Greg, I also get homesick, but you have to realize all the things you've gained that you would never have gotten had you stayed here."

His comments were extremely sobering, as I had never considered the chances I was given by my mum and dad, who left their own lives and families behind in their decision to move their children away to another country for a chance at a life much better than the one given to us. Hearing these words from the mouth of my mate, and hearing about his own life moving on in a different direction, was a wake-up call for me. I had to let go of my mourning for home. But it also allowed me the chance to look back on many of the experiences I was granted while growing up in Canada that I would never have had if I had stayed in Northern Ireland. I had to stop torturing myself with the "what if" perspectives.

Over the years, and as my daughter reminded me, my love of music provided me with countless opportunities to meet with bands and actually work for them as well. This included being a part of the local crew for Pink Floyd's *The Division Bell* world tour, which made a stop in Winnipeg at the stadium on Canada Day – July 1, 1994. This was followed up with the Rolling Stones *Voodoo Lounge* tour on August 23, 1994, as well as U2's *PopMart* tour on June 12, 1997. Each of these was a ten-day stint and was an incredible stage production to be a part of.

While I was attending South Winnipeg Technical College in 1994, I had a chance to do a phone interview with Dick Massey, who played the role of Billy "The Animal" Mooney in the movie *The Commitments* based on the novel by Roddy Doyle. It was by all accounts a great discussion, as Dick was very accommodating in answering my questions. The band was touring in support of the success from the movie soundtrack that included a stop at the Walker Theatre.

Robert Arkins, who played the band's manager in the movie as Jimmy "The Bollocks" Rabbitte; and Kenneth McCluskey, who played the role of Derek "Meatman" Scully, were part of the tour. They gave me the chance to meet them backstage after the show and were interested in meeting my siblings as well. The craic between us all—being from Dublin and Belfast, along with the rest of the group—indeed made for a memorable night.

Another memorable experience was working with Garth Brooks during his 1996 *Fresh Horses* tour, where he played three sold-out shows August 17, 18, and 19 at the Winnipeg arena. This was a very different event for me, as I was never a fan of country music. Yet here I would be working for one of the world's largest icons in that industry.

I was amazed at his interactive play with the audience, who hung on to and sung each word to every song along with him. He invited fans to bring cameras along with them to his shows. For the first two concert nights, I was assigned to work the stage left of the arena on the floor seating area. In front of my walkway were three rows of chairs, then from the fourth row to about the fifteenth row I could roam back and forth to ensure fans stayed in their seats.

What I had caught on to though was that a number of young kids decked out in their best cowboy or cowgirl outfits were trying to take pictures from their chairs by standing on them, but we had a policy not to do so. They were politely asked to sit down as to not block other concertgoers' view. I have no idea what inspired me to do this, but I started to walk as far back as the fifteenth row of chairs and would ask kids within my section to walk up with me to the third row so they could capture better memories.

After bringing the first few up and being told by my boss that they would only be allowed one picture each, I brought a child of about five or six years of age up from the back row to the same section for his opportunity of a lifetime. However, due to his small stature, I could tell he was struggling to get a shot, as Garth was standing in the middle of the stage.

Without thinking, I put my hands under the arms of this young child, thrust him straight up into the air, and while locking my arms told him, "Take as many shots as you can while you're up there."

Seeing this child floating in the air with his camera clicking away at the hands of one of the security guards, Garth Brooks made his way across stage left, stopped directly in front of me, leaned out across the audience, and played his guitar while singing to this child. My arms were growing weak, so after countless pictures had been taken, I put the child back down and told him to go back to his seat.

Meanwhile, another child who was maybe ten or eleven years of age came darting up to me in hopes of getting the same opportunity. I did exactly that, but unfortunately could not hold him up as long. I heard a "pop" and realized that my arm has jumped out of its socket. The child did indeed get his pictures before going back to his seat. At this time, I was left standing and looking directly at Garth Brooks, who reached his pick hand out, made the "thumbs up" sign directly at me, and nodded acknowledgement of what I had done to make the night of two kids extremely memorable, along with the countless other kids I brought up to the third row to get pictures of their idol. This night was for them. I merely helped.

The third night of the show, I was assigned to the backstage left exit ramp and had the most amazing opportunity to watch the show come together. Garth and his band played their set, and before going back on stage for the first of his encores, he came off the stage at my secure area. I pointed a flashlight for him and referred to him as Mr. Brooks. But what amazed me was his kindness not only to me as a local hired hand, but that people who had brought clothes to the show for his newborn daughter Allie were taken by his tour crew and presented to him backstage. I stood and watched in awe as he toweled himself off while inspecting every article of clothing and saying how much he appreciated these gifts and gestures by his expansive fan base. After this, he gulped down a bottle of water and got ready to go back on stage. Prior to the show, he had also met with our entire security team and signed as many autographs and took as many photographs as possible, saying that he appreciated *our* efforts before and during his shows.

One of my more significant and up-close experiences includes one night with alt-rocker Marilyn Manson when he stopped at the Walker Theatre on July 28, 1997. I was working with a firm that provided concert security. We were briefed before the show that we were not to speak to him, nor were we allowed to look him in the eyes.

My assigned position for that night was the stage left door to allow the band to both enter and exit the stage. We were not prepared for the antics that are often spoken about, which included a fan who scaled the outside wall of the venue on a drainpipe and got dragged into the dressing room for his efforts.

I managed to catch a few songs from behind the scenes, but what I was not prepared for was that after putting on an extremely exhaustive set list and exiting the stage accompanied by his personal bodyguard, Marilyn Manson collapsed on top of me. I had nowhere to go. I looked down towards my feet and thought, "Holy Jesus. Marilyn Manson's lying on my feet. What the hell am I supposed to do?"

I simply stood there. Due to the circumstances of the events that were now unfolding, I ignored the order that we had been given before the show and looked down at a rocker who both inspired and infuriated the world with his on- and off-stage antics as well as his music as he stared back up at me. It was not my job to judge him. I had to wait while he got himself sorted out.

★★★★★

Recent events in Northern Ireland left me pausing to reflect further, and cemented within my mind what Denis had told me after being away for twenty-five years. Bonefires once again raged across Belfast and neighbouring enclaves. This only ignites the hatred once again and further divides the community in half.

There have been reports in countless headlines which are also online, including photographed images of a statue of the Virgin

Mary being placed on top of a fire to burn after the face of it had been smashed, only to be rescued by local community leaders who had sense to see the destruction this causes. They gave it to a nearby church.

Other images show an effigy of the Pope at the very top waiting to be incinerated along with everything else that has been placed on the carefully stacked rows of wooden pallets. The images are a pathetic reminder of the bitter place Northern Ireland became while I was growing up there during this time of year.

I would hope that the mindless actions of a select minority do not speak for a majority of people. I have countless friends from both sides who, like ourselves, choose to not be a part of this barbaric, mindless violence. Instead, they leave the North of Ireland before, during, and after this time, which for whatever reason is called a "celebration," and take themselves off elsewhere in the country to enjoy time with family, friends, or to get away from the bigotry that is openly displayed and passed down from one generation to the next.

A celebration usually involves good food and the gathering of people from all walks of life coming together as ONE to enjoy in their event, without leaving behind scars of loathsome hatred, which only throws Belfast and its surrounding communities back into a state of utter pandemonium.

How exactly does my country hope to ever move forward and bring people from all over the world to this nation? This nation could be great because of the people that live here, the craic, the banter, the culture, and the vibrancy of the nightlife, as well as the breathtaking scenery found throughout the six counties in the North. Yet when these destructive events and behaviours occur time and time again and are broadcast on social media, television, and radio stations across the world, I have to ask: who wants or needs it except for a select number of individuals?

I have spoken with countless people who would love to tour Ireland both North and South, but choose to stay in the South as to not be exposed to all the rubbish. Therefore, I wonder if there is still a belief out there that people from various nations worldwide come to celebrate actions of revulsion, prejudice, torment, and hostility, especially when the flag from their country is also being desecrated and publicly displayed before being set ablaze on the eleventh night.

I ask what the reason behind this is? It is not in the name of religion, which is often used as the excuse behind the hatred. It is not in the name of politics. It is not in the name of world freedom. It is in the name of hatred, persecution, and the downright display of one's ignorance, for which I am so glad that twenty-eight years ago, my mum and dad had the insight and the fortitude to leave everything behind in order to bring my siblings and I out of that environment of human decline. Who wants it? And who needs it?

The Irish are known for St. Patrick's Day, which is celebrated the world over. I do not see this creating hatred or dividing communities except in and around Belfast. Thus, I can only hope that there will be a day—perhaps but unlikely within my lifetime—that I see Northern Ireland make a drastic change in what should be deemed a celebration for all people to participate in.

Denis's comments allowed me the chance to realize that I have been given more than my fair share of opportunity to do and experience things that many others haven't, for which I should be eternally grateful. A jammie bastard indeed.

# Brandy

I CAN TRULY SAY I do not understand why life can be so cruel by throwing us into emotional roller coaster rides. Just when we think we are on top of the world, life squarely punches us in the gut. In my case, life had a seek-and-destroy targeting system locked squarely onto me.

After writing the final segments of this book, making the necessary edits and arranging the publication processes with my publisher, I felt I had the world in my hands. I was on cloud nine. After three long years of writing this book, I would finally realize my dream. Contracts were drawn up. All I had left to do was submit the completed manuscript in its entirety.

Regardless of my happiness, I was about to be proved wrong in that there was another reflection just waiting to be written. Brandy...

I had to say goodbye to my beloved pet dog, Brandy McVicker, who has been with me for the past sixteen years of my life. She was born May 1, 1996, and celebrated her most recent birthday as a senior citizen a few short months ago. Not

even a week before, I had done some research to look at her lifespan, which on average is twelve to fourteen years. She was seventeen. By all accounts, she was well past the average age, although this past year was difficult regarding her health.

Her breed is that of a Kooikerhondje or a Kooiker Hound, which I understand hails from Amsterdam. I never did get the correct pronunciation of her breed. Instead, she was Brandy. My furry friend was called "Brandy Fluffytoes," by my mum, as when her hair grew out and she went to the groomer, it was as if someone had literally taken a pair of crimping tongs to her entire body and gave her a wrinkly hairdo.

This breed of animal is loving and beautiful in colour, personality, and friendship. Their loyalty to those who are blessed enough to have one is unmatched. Brandy was playful and gentle. She loved kids and would give a knowing bark to protect her property, but if given the chance, she would simply come up, and while checking a person over before realizing if she knew them, would run all over the place with a tail that wagged like an oversized feather duster.

She had a sensitive patch of sorts on her back, which the Humane Society explained was like a nervous twitch. When patted or scratched in this area, she would quite literally wag her back and whole fluffy bum, almost dancing in the air while giving a low but non-threatening growl. The sight of this was cute, as it was like she was doing her own breakdance.

Being an asthmatic, I have had several allergies to animals for years, specifically cats. There are also many breeds of dogs that affect and leave me with watering eyes, wheezy breathing, and a stuffy nose. So on that spring day in May of 1997, I stopped in at the Winnipeg Humane Society to enquire about adopting a pet that would hopefully be suitable.

Behind the counter and running around, panting excitedly while checking everything out was a beautiful golden and pure white dog with amber eyes. She was brought in that day since her previous owner could not keep her as they were moving to an apartment. I enquired about her, but they had a twenty-four hour clause that all animals had to go through in order to judge their suitability for adults, children, and with other pets before they could be considered for adoption. Thus she was not available at that time.

The next day I went back and asked about Brandy. She was not behind the counter but if I wanted to give her consideration, I had until 6pm to secure her. I placed a down payment to put her on hold, otherwise she would be released for someone else to consider.

Cats and dogs of all shapes, sizes, breeds, and colours were within their caged areas, some making their presence known with loud meows and barks. My daughter Caitlin and I walked along, seeing all of the puppy dog eyes looking back at us before we came upon Brandy with the word "hold" written on her cage. She was not barking. She was not making her presence known or pacing all over, checking out her surroundings. as she had been the night before when I had first seen her. She was sitting behind the caged door, her head down and amber eyes so sad that when we stopped and lowered ourselves, she lifted her paw to us as if to say, "I'm sorry for doing something wrong, but I don't know what that was. Here's my paw. Would you please give me a second chance or take me home?"

My heart melted while sounds of "Awww" left me. This beautiful animal showed her charm from the first time we laid eyes on her.

There was no doubt in my mind that she would be coming home with us, although my allergies had to be put to the test as well as our suitability to adopt.

We waited in the family area while a staff member went to retrieve Brandy. She came out, tail wagging, panting with excited joy that someone had come to visit. We checked her out. Caitlin and I patted her soft coat and decided to take her for a walk. She was utterly ecstatic by this decision and extremely happy to get out of her caged confines.

We brought Brandy back to the centre and took an hour to sit with her. The staff kept asking how I was feeling. Did my allergies flare up? Was I stuffy? How were my eyes? They knew from our discussions that cats and other pets took a huge toll on me. For days I would suffer after coming into contact with them. However, nothing had happened during the time we spent with her, but I wanted to be sure. If we were to adopt Brandy, one more test was required. I guess this would have to be called the "Face in Fur" test, as I did just that and buried my face in her soft hair

Brandy, beside Ciarán when he was twenty-one months old in his play castle. I taught Brandy to jump up onto the first platform before she made her way up to the second platform as is seen here.

to see how I would trigger. This was the do-or-die moment, and with my allergies being as severe as they were, this could have become the latter for me.

We waited. And waited. And waited… There was nothing to trigger. Obviously my timing the night before was a genuine sign that Brandy was going to come home with us that day, which she did.

We signed her papers and made sure that all of her shots were up to date before bringing our excited fur ball home for the first time. We stopped at the pet shop to get a leash, collar, bowl, food, toys, bones, a brush, and anything else we could think of that our beloved girl would need.

She loved the car ride with the window open, panting while sniffing at the outside air and traveling to her new place of residence, one that was not filled with barking dogs, five-by-eight foot caged fences, or were she had to lift her front paw into the air to seek forgiveness.

Caitlin was only three at the time Brandy joined us in 1997, whereas my son Ciarán was introduced to her at birth. She was a huge part of our family.

She celebrated Christmas with us. She went for walks to the local Diary Queen for a small bowl of ice cream topped by a doggie biscuit while we enjoyed our sundaes. She would join us at the park and would check everything out with her finely tuned and inquisitive nose. She loved going to the beach to frolic in the water before shaking her wet coat all over us.

In the past year, Brandy's health started to seriously decline on me. I noticed she was growing thin compared to her healthy fifty-nine-pound self. She was rapidly losing weight. At last weigh in, when I placed her on the scale, I almost choked when it read thirty-nine pounds. My poor Brandyfluff was deteriorating quickly, and there was nothing I could do.

I made a second trip back to the vet a week later as she just was not herself. I was prepared at that time to go ahead and euthanize my beloved girl, letting her go and freeing her from whatever disease was robbing her body of its nutrients, tissue, fat, and muscle. It was believed to be cancer. Thankfully, as she was already on antibiotics I was not forced to go through with this horrible and most certainly difficult choice. I made the decision right there and then to keep her as comfortable as possible and in a palliative form, trying to look after her as best I could while spending whatever days she had left with my kids and I.

**My beloved dog, Brandy, who brought us sixteen years of unconditional love and friendship. She is sorely missed.**

On a hot, sunny July 4th and after returning home from work, I walked in to find Brandy in a deep, almost coma-like sleep. She seemed to be becoming more and more like this; she scared me many a morning when I would get out of bed to check on her, not knowing whether she had passed away during the night on her bed or blanket. I called her and when she finally woke, it was obvious that her condition had deteriorated even further on me. She was very confused. Her poor eyes and ears had not been functioning in the attentive way they once did, while her sense of her surroundings had become strange to her. She pawed the kitchen floor, seeking the step that would take her out the back door onto the flat landing before she would have to navigate three more steps into the garden.

I had to help her across the kitchen, and it was obvious the disease within her body was very much making its ugly presence known. I helped her to the first step while gently bringing her along and giving her time to hopefully find her surroundings. She made it outside and, after chancing the first of three steps, paused.

I encouraged her to come down one step at a time, but when she was ready. Although it was obviously a struggle, she managed this and checked out the garden area, a routine she did daily to see what other pets had passed by and tagged her favourite corner.

During this time, I went into the house to bring out a few recyclables while Brandy followed me slowly down the garden path and waited for me. The once boundless ball of energy she was had come to slowed movements, although her bark would still let people know she was there and was watching them as best as she could.

She came back up the steps for a drink of water I had placed to quench her thirst while I went back into the house. I checked her food bowl. It was full from that morning, as her food intake was very sporadic and becoming difficult to manage. What I did not realize is that she had gone back out the garden to take in a shaded area and lie down...

I got to her as she was taking her final breaths. Screaming hysterically at the top of my lungs, I picked Brandy up, carried her over to a flat patio area, and started to give her the kiss of life. I was determined to not lose my beloved dog. This was not her time to go.

Frantically begging her to stay with me in between administering whatever air was in my lungs into hers, I tried cupping water in my hands and placing it over her nose and mouth so she could have something to drink. But my efforts were not to be successful. My beloved pet of sixteen years died in my arms at seventeen years, two months, and three days of age. My Brandy was free from her suffering. She was free of the disease that was slowly stealing her gift of life away from me. She was free from caged bars, barking dogs, and noisy cars. She gained her independence on the same day American's celebrate theirs.

In the midst of this chaos, I had my mobile phone to my ear, screaming frantically and asking for help. Our cherished pet now lay lifeless below me, her body still warm. It was a matter of trying to figure out how tell my kids that their beloved Brandy had passed away.

While waiting for my kids to come over, I posted photos of Brandy on a social media site to announce her passing with a short obituary of sorts, trying to seek comfort in the support of friends. Once I hit the send button, however, I had to go back outside to my pet. My dear friend Ruth McDonald, who

The Kiss Me Kate flower that my sister Angela had planted, which bloomed on one side the same day that Brandy would be leaving me.

is halfway through her degree to become an animal technician, provided a ton of support. Ruth, your dedication to address the needs of our furry friends when they are sick goes beyond merit of description and for which I am so grateful.

My kids found me slumped over her body, sobbing uncontrollably and petting her like we had done for so many years all the wile holding onto her and not ever wanting to let her go. Four hearts broke that night. A number of signs seemed to come into play throughout the day but certainly did not prepare me for the events that evening. This enhanced my spiritual belief that we are constantly given reminders in life that are not coincidental, but as a warning for us to prepare ourselves for the unexpected.

Upon arriving home that day, a rose bush my sister Angela had planted many years before had stopped blooming and had only come back to life in the last two years. It is called a "Kiss Me Kate," which Angela said was for our mum. As I walked up the pathway prior to finding Brandy in her almost coma-like state of sleep, I noticed that one of the two flower buds had bloomed in full. "Mum is here with me," I thought before going into the house.

During the day I had been working on what I thought was my final submission for this book entitled "Hallows Eve," as I needed to get the introduction to it written. Once all of this was done, and while laying out the actual format of this book and trying to make it all flow and fit together, I looked through the contents section and "The Pulse of Derrylin" caught my eye. I went back to the end of this composition and added my dedication to John McManus, Sr., along with that of Tommy and Valerie. But I have often heard that death comes in threes. Maybe this was a sign that death was once again to pass over my doorstep later that evening.

After my kids and I said our farewells, we would need to get Brandy over to the animal hospital for final preparations. I laid out her blanket, which I had only just finished washing and put on the deck to dry rather than throwing it into the dryer. I very gently placed her warm, lifeless body on her blanket for the last time.

We said more goodbyes as I folded the material around her but left her head exposed, as if hoping the night air would bring her back to life. My hopes were in vain while I carried her to my car as if she were a baby.

Slowly and with my kids in tow, we placed our beloved pet in the back seat for one last journey and opened the windows for her as I had always done when she went out for car rides. I was saddened and angry at the same time, speaking through clenched teeth.

While en route to the animal hospital, Caitlin informed me that as I was lifting Brandy for her final journey, a group of kids who were cycling by happened to be playing a very specific song by one of her favourite bands called Simple Plan. The song is "Summer Paradise," which made her reflect on the meaning of the lyric that played.

Reflecting in my mind while talking out loud, I shared with Caitlin the signs I had seen that day but without truly understanding what they meant. Just then, we both reached back to hold onto our pet as our car drove way below the speed limit, delaying the inevitable we would have to face upon our arrival.

We spent another hour with our beloved pet. Our family member who for sixteen years gave us unconditional friendship; who wanted nothing more than to wag her tail and run up and down the pathway when we came home; who met us at the door and would check out the groceries we bought by sticking her inquisitive nose into each bag to see what was for her or what she could get into; who brought undying love to our family unit as only a dog knows how to do.

It was during our time at home while prepping Brandy and in saying our final farewells that I decided she would forever be memorialized within the pages of this book, and that I would need to write a reflection to her memory for all she brought into our lives. We decided to have her privately cremated so that her ashes would come home and remain with us in a sandstone urn. Caitlin and I looked at a chart and felt the most appropriate, being reflective of our Irish heritage (even though Brandy's breed is from Amsterdam), would have to be green. Even in death, it certainly brings together a collection of cultures.

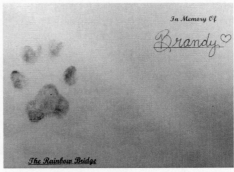

Brandy's final paw print, as was captured on the night of her passing.

The following morning was a total blur. I phoned the vet and asked if I could make special arrangements to have a second print of her paw done. Call it a coping mechanism, part of the grieving process, or a mark of respect. We all grieve and celebrate the life and death of a loved one in our own ways.

This poem was shared with my daughter and I last night as we grieved over Brandy. The author is unknown, but it captures a beauty that describes what I hope she is experiencing right now, away from the disease that robbed her from us.

There is a bridge connecting Heaven and Earth. It is called the Rainbow Bridge because of its many colors. Just this side of the Rainbow Bridge there is a land of meadows, hills, and valleys with lush green grass. When a pet dies, the pet goes to this place. There is always food, water, and warm spring weather. The old and frail animals are young again. The abandoned animals are again surrounded by friends. Those who are maimed are whole again. They play the whole day, every day, with each other. There is only one thing missing. They are not with their special people who loved them here on earth. So, each day they run and play until the day comes when one suddenly stops playing and looks up. The nose twitches! The ears perk up! The eyes water! And, suddenly this one pet bolts excitedly away from the other animals! Your pet has seen you arrive! And when you meet your special friend again, you take him or her in your arms and embrace. Your face and nose and lips and neck are licked again and again and again... and you look once more into those soulful eyes of your loving pet. And then, holding each other, you cross the Rainbow Bridge together... never again to be separated.

**Brandy McVicker**
**May 01, 1996 – July 04, 2013**
**A MAN'S BEST FRIEND!**

Brandy, this is for you kiddo. I can't wait to see you healthy and free again someday when my name whispers in the breeze, sweetie. Thank you for sixteen wonderful years. You were one in a million. You were my best friend in triumph and tribulation, but never passed judgment. You greeted me with a loving wag of your fluffy tail and panted happily when I came home from work each day. My heart weeps for you. Goodbye for now, my beloved friend. I'll see you in time...

# With Love from an Irish Mother

IRISH MOTHERS HAVE very endearing qualities. My mum was brilliant at using wee sayings against my brother, two sisters and me, but would sometimes get tripped up in her words. In our teen years, this would come back full circle to haunt her. For the sake of talking, if she needed me to do something to help her out or that she needed to speak to me, she would go through the full roster of our names but not in chronological order. She would begin by calling out "Joseph, Angela, Karen," and would finally get it right but on occasion it would be the F word that was called before she found my name, followed by Jesus, Mary, and Joseph. I would explain that Jesus and Mary didn't live in our house, and would get scolded for doing so.

In her later years, my mum was almost crippled with rheumatoid arthritis. One day I told her the reason for her trouble was that she had threatened my siblings and me that if we did not do as we were told, she would "put her toe up our holes." Thankfully, she laughed at this.

The Irish are famous for the lilt in our brogues and the friendliness in our approach to welcoming visitors coming to tour our wee country, including showing them the sights, sounds, and hundreds of pubs during a crawl or the laid-back way of our lifestyle. Those of us from the North also enjoy this when we are not trying to half kill one another. But the sayings we have in Belfast can leave a person both shocked and laughing uncontrollably at what it is that comes out of our gubs—especially when said by our mas!

In my childhood years there were more than enough times that I came home from school and asked my ma what was for dinner. Her response would often be, "Shite and sugar." I was one of the fussiest eaters on this planet. My ma became annoyed with me asking what was for dinner, as she knew I'd screw up my nose at it after she'd spent all day working over a hot stove and preparing a meal.

What I've learned through the connection of social media is that many children who were reared throughout Northern Ireland were subjected to what some may consider the same harsh tongue that our mas can have—or as they would prefer to tell us, terms of endearment. This is a very true statement, with the slight exception of being called a "parcel of wee bastards" for our actions and behaviours over the years. I'm sure we weren't alone.

My granny would often come around to visit or we would go to her house. I would watch in awe at how her conversation with my mum would go on forever, without either one of them ever stopping to take a breath. "Right, c'meredya tell ya. Say's I. Say's he. Aye. Say's I 'til her. And she says 'til me. Aye, and here's me…" I always marveled at how they did this. Somehow, I fully understood where the conversation was going.

I was about seven-years-old when my granny was up at our house visiting my ma. Again, I would watch, as my granny would say, "Kathleen C'mere 'til I tell ya." While saying that, she would be reaching for my mums wrist or arm, and had to touch it as if to prevent my mum from running away.

I had a common cold on the go and was sitting on the couch, minding my own business and watching TV while both my ma and my granny were sitting on chairs in the living room chatting to each other.

I looked to my ma and said, "Mummy, my nose is running." Without blinking an eye she simply responded, "Well, get up and close the door to keep it in."

I pulled my arse off the couch, closed the door that separated our living room from the hallway, and sat back down. In my young mind this could have been the perfect remedy to cure my sniffles. I certainly could not understand why my granny and ma had bust into fits of laughter at my actions, as we'd been instructed over the years to "do as yer told and don't defy me."

Being the third youngest sibling, I often found myself getting a diggin' from my older brother Joe. The saying was that "boys will be boys," but I would go running to my ma to complain about his latest bashing. She became fed up with us, and rather than come to my rescue, would shout, "Ack, quit yer gurnin' would'je? If you don't stop, I'll give you somethin' to gurn about. You're like a bloody Christmas card so you are – always greetin'."

This was one way Irish mothers tried to toughen up their kids and make them stand on their own two feet while learning to fight their own battles, as life on the streets was less than a tiptoe through the daisies. Regardless of her efforts, it didn't save me from getting my arse kicked on a regular basis or my head bashed into the bedroom wall almost every night while I slept.

Some of the other sayings she came off with are ones she'd tell her grandchildren after we began having our own wee families. As such, our children grew up learning the fabric and culture of our language, but seemingly much less harshly than what we were accustomed too.

As thousands around the world whose roots originate in Ireland can attest, the Irish are storytellers and have a unique way of sharing their thoughts. We call them "wee stories," a "bit of craic and banter," or "havin' ye on." Now although this is the way we were raised, if she did not agree with what she was hearing, my ma would look us straight in the eyes and say, "You're full of mad dog's shite," "Your heads cut," or "Away and give my head peace." We would also hear, "You're full of hobby horse's shite," or "Yer arse is out the windy." A windy is our description of a window, but don't ask me why my arse was out there in the first place.

"God curse and roast yis' all," or other much more slanderous terms were not uncommon either, as my sisters, brother, and me were by no means Charlie's angels (although we let on to be since that is my da's first name). We were often asked, "Where do ya think youse are, your daddy's yacht?"

Regardless of our repeated attempts, there was no escaping my ma's sixth sense, even though she warned us repeatedly that she had eyes on the back of her head. Perhaps that is why we lovingly named her "Katie the Spud Lady," and maybe a bit of a better explanation as to why we ourselves were labeled in a variety of colourful ways.

Some of her other favourite sayings included, "Ack. Your bum's a plum," or "Yer heads a marley." Those are just a wee sample of some of the things my ma would come off with. I've since realized she was not the only one who spoke like this to her kids.

I wondered what it was like for others who grew up around the same time as me. I decided to launch a Facebook page to promote this book in advance of its launch. Interaction has been steadily increasing with "Likes." Those who've come to the page have been enjoying photos and reflections, as well as sharing their own wee anecdotes of years gone by. And so, I put a post online that read as follows:

How many of you were faced with these sayings as heard from an Irish mother?

Kids: "What's for dinner?"
Ma: "Shite and sugar on it."
Kids: "My nose is runnin'."
Ma: "Well close the door and keep it in."
Kids: "He's hurtin' me."
Ma: "Ack, quit yer gurning, will ye?"
Kids: (Generally being cheeky).
Ma: "I'll put my toe up your hole."
Kids: (telling a wee yarn).

Ma: "Ack, your bums a plum!"
Any others out there you care to share?

The response was phenomenal and completely beyond my wildest expectations. It went viral, as those who are part of the Belfast Child Facebook page posted memories and shared these reflections outwards with the online community.

What I was happy to find out though is that my sisters, brother, and me were not the only ones who were regularly told that supper would consist of "Shite and sugar," as a lady who shares my mum's name, Catherine, said this was offered as a choice of meal at her house too. Perhaps she's a long-lost relative?

Susie and Mary were told that supper consisted of "stewed bugs with onions," or "bulls balls with onions," only to inform their mas neither of them liked onions, but missing the primary ingredients! Thankfully Leanne explained that this was actually minced meat served with carrots. As far back as I can remember, this was never offered as a menu item in our house although "stewed bugs" does sound much more appetizing and palatable than shite.

William got a healthier diet, as his ma would offer him "strips of daylight and vinegar," while Chrissy got a bit of a different selection that included "sheep's shite and water grass." Martin ended up with a foreign dish called "Nannygoats' nibbies." Glenda was offered a few additional choices, as she shared, "We got 'hell roast ye!' when we did somethin' wrong, and for dinner it was 'sheep shite and onions,' or 'fadge and hen dung." Mealtimes within homes around Ireland were quite interesting.

One thing about Irish mothers, is that they have an affinity for using body parts to describe their children, including making specific reference to their heads. Catriona told me that her ma would say, "If you'd brains, you'd be dangerous," while Tracey echoed that comment with, "There's more brains in a false face."

Karen shared that our own wee ma would tell us, "If you'd two brains, you'd be twice as thick," although I also recall her telling me in the most loving and affectionate manner, "If your brains were made of dynamite, you couldn't part your hair."

My ma was a very proud woman and proud of her kids, and if we weren't groomed to her very high personal standards, she would do a full head inspection. While combing us over she would say, "Would you look at the dirt in those ears? You could grow spuds in them." That statement always terrified me. Potatoes were very much a natural part of the Irish diet, and I certainly didn't want to eat them mashed, boiled, or roasted if it meant they were coming from within my own two ears.

Our mothers had the best interests of their children's facial features in mind but used a variety of ways to describe and protect them. Beth's reflected, "Get them hands out of your pocket or if you fall you'll have nothing to save your feace." Imelda shared, "My ma would say if a gust of wind comes, yer feace'll stay like that." As told by Ann, "If you die with a face like that, the undertaker wouldn't wash it." Now if that's not a term of endearment, I don't know what is.

Our noses come next. Simon Kerr, who hails from my neighbourhood, agreed about the protective measures our mothers had by telling us, "If you keep picking your nose like that, your head'll cave in." Kathleen expanded that thought by sharing, "When she sees a child picking its nose, my ma says 'when ya get to the bridge, give us a wave.'"

Katrina recounted a term many of us would have heard throughout our childhood years: "Quit picking your willick!" Teresa's ma would say, "Will ya be diggin' there the mara?" before saying, "The snatters are trippin' ye." This was one of the most common sayings we heard before a clump of bog roll would be dragged across our faces, removing several layers of skin in the process.

Reading through all of the comments online made me reflect in awe how our mas could tell us these things with such grace and eloquence, all the while keeping a straight face while looking in our immediate direction and without batting an eyelash.

Sticking with the topic of facial features, Trish shared, "My ma would always say to me 'you've a mouth on you like the Cave Hill'," while Teresa would be told, "You've a mouth like Portsmouth," which is located in the Southern part of England. Several naval vessels dock there.

We knew where we stood as children, as Annmarie would be told, "Away you out en play; yer like yer ma's apron strings," while Margaret reflected, "My ma was always sayin' 'Yer like my arse; you're a bit of a bum.'" My own mum would tell us, "Ack, away and eat one of me arses, will ye?" I never did understand how she thought she'd more than one arse.

The other mechanism our mums used to keep us in our places was the threat of violence. Pat wrote about his experiences and shared, "If I hurt myself and came in crying, my ma used to say 'I'll give ya something to cry for.' We were given no sympathy." Maria added to that by writing, "You'll be laughing on the other side of your feace if I have to come up there," in reference to sorting kids who were "actin' a maggot."

Christine further expanded upon this: "You'll know your arse from yer elbow when I get me hands on ya!" Talk about baptism by fire, as Michelle shared that her ma would say, "If you don't learn to close them doors I am going to trap your fingers in them and then you won't forget."

Michelle went on to post a back and forth engagement with her ma:

"What's wrong wifya?"

"I'm dying."

"Well, go and die a bit quieter somewhere else then and give my head peace, would'ja?"

My mum would tell me this as well but would include, "You'd drive a bloody saint to drink, so you would." At least he'd be in good company with Bloody Mary once he got to the Cloud 9 pub.

The threat of perceived violence was very much a common thread among many Irish households, since we were offered several beatings to keep us in our places. Dorothy wrote, "Come in here 'til I belt you one and if you don't come now, it'll be twice as bad when you do." Catherine also noted from her upbringing that, "When being naughty, we got threatened with the wooden spoon, belt, or slipper…"

My own mum would say, "Do you want a thick ear?" As she had suggested this to me on so many occasions, I thought one day I would take her up on it and responded, "Aye, I would," at which she point she said to me, "Don't be so friggin' cheeky or I'll put my toe squarely up your hole!" I guess she was giving me an alternative, but it still does not answer that age-old question: how do you fit a square peg into a round object?

Even when asking for help, my sister Karen reminded me that we were always told, "You're big enough and ugly enough to do it yourself." In looking back, I should have enquired what side of the family those genes came from. However, if it meant my ma coming back at me with, "D'ya see when I get a howlayee wee lad? I'm going to knock your melt in for yer cheek." An important lesson learned is that silence speaks volumes and one should choose their "ma battles" carefully.

The point of no return was finally reached when, after we had done everything possible to drive them up the wall, hundreds upon thousands of Irish mothers would bring out their most secretive, most destructive, and most deadly weapon of mass destruction. They'd utter six words that would invade our spud-filled ears and stop us dead in our tracks:

"Wait 'til your father gets home."

Karen, Joe, Angela, and I knew then and there that life was about to change for us in an extremely drastic manner. The damage from us testing and pushing the limits along with our insufferable behaviour was irreparable. We succeeded in our attempts to drive our ma over the cliff.

With those dreaded words, it was as if the imperial march theme from the Star Wars film *The Empire Strikes Back* began playing while we awaited the arrival of Darth Vader himself…

### *"Greg… search your feelings… I'm yer da!"*

My father spent the first fifteen years of my life at sea, and so for about two or three weeks out of every year, he'd come home. That was the only time we'd see him. It was also the signal of doomsday for us all.

Our ma had corresponded all the years he was away by pen and paper and wrote several letters each and every month to him. My da, on the other hand, with his methodical and intricate system of keeping every file, pay stub, or piece or correspondence he's ever received since he was a child (he maintains this pattern to this very day), would save these letters and bring them all home in his suitcase when he was granted leave.

Of course the first night was always brilliant for us to see him, as my mum would bring my siblings and me on what seemed to be the long, arduous drive over to Larne. We'd stand there and wait for the Sealink Ferry to get in, watching him disembark from the gangplank, all the while being bloody freezing as the Irish coastal winds cut us to the bone.

We'd make our way home again, excited for whatever presents he had picked up from the various ports he stopped at during his voyages. My da would go out and come back with a tin of Coke, a packet of crisps, and a chocolate bar for each of us from the Beverly shops at the bottom of the Carnmoney road. As there was an off-license there, he could buy himself a few tins of beer and a wee bottle of scotch for our ma, along with a couple of bars of Cadbury Fruit and Nut. We couldn't have been happier with the gifts we received and our spoils of sweets, which we would stuff our faces with.

The magic continued, as we were given a chance to stay up a little bit later and granted the opportunity to try and take advantage of the situation by using our endearing Irish charms against our da, who was now very much at home with us all. Yet those words of mass destruction my ma had threatened us with still rang out like church bells within our heads…

The four of us crawled all over him, praying our efforts at affection would help soothe away from his memory all of the bad behaviours my ma had captured within those countless letters. We'd use every single trick a Belfast child could think of against their father in the hopes that he wouldn't beat us half to death.

No matter our efforts, and although written well after our time as children but to use this wonderful analogy created by one of my most favourite of authors, J.K. Rowling, we could not summon the brilliance of Hermione Granger or Harry Potter and use a Time Turner to go back in time to make all of our wrongs right. Simply using our fingers and pointing an imaginary wand at his suitcase while uttering the words, "*Accio ma's letters*" would not work either. And although there were times that thoughts had drifted through my mind of running to his suitcase and eating those letters if it meant escaping a perilous death, I couldn't muster up the courage, as that would have led to a fate worse than what was already in store for us all.

We had to resort to giving him kisses on his stubbly face, as he hadn't shaved before coming home but that was more like trying to snog a hedgehog. In our minds, our measures of subtly planning how we were hopefully not going to have to plead our cases in front of the judge, jury, and executioner, had seemingly paid off. Our charms and affections worked. We were happy, as was my da. Life was brilliant.

But then it was time to meet our maker. Our plans died with the night's sleep.

On the first Saturday morning he was home, due to his own sea schedule and during the waking hours of the dead, my da would drag our weary arses out of bed instead of allowing us a wee lie-in a bit longer within our toasty kips. Our bed sheets were torn clean from our bodies while we lay shivering, trying to shake off the sleep and focus on what was happening. "C'mon, get up, you've got work to do," followed our rude awakening.

We were not allowed any cartoons. No speaking while the BBC news was on. And if the school lockers he had built for us were not immaculate by naval standards (even though we did our best to keep them clean), our belongings would end up out in the front garden for us to go fetch in our pajamas and bare feet, as our guddies were also out in the garden!

Our friends didn't need to watch cartoons either, and they could have actually saved their parents from buying a TV license by simply gathering on the front street while watching our belongings flying through the air. This would be followed by four skinny wee friggers fighting among themselves as to who owned what, scavenging to pick up their school supplies and incomplete homework assignments.

There was no mercy from Lord Vader. He did not need to bring his thumb and forefinger together almost in a pinch with his arm outstretched, using his dark Jedi mind power against us and taking deep breaths. Just the very sound of his voice, the look in his steely eyes, and the dark hair on his arms was enough to frighten the shite out of us all! Thankfully he did not have the use of a

Lightsaber, otherwise we'd all have been struck down and our crumpled cloaks would have ended up in the front garden, along with the rest of our belongings.

Now before you think I'm being dreadful here with my comments and giving my da a terrible slagging—or as our Karen so lovingly refers to him, Chuckie Our Da—I want to let you know I am not alone in my thoughts about the threat of him coming home.

Briege reflected, "I always remember 'wait until your da gets in.' Fekin scary that was." In addition, Carol gave a little bit more insight as to what her experiences were like by writing, "It was always after Mum beat you for doing something wrong then she'd say 'wait till your dad gets home; see what you get then' and believe me, you got another wallop." I guess the empire really did strike back!

In saying all that and giving a wee salute to our fathers (and no, I do not mean the ones recited kneeling beside our beds, gazing at the ceiling, and bringing our hands together before laying ourselves down to sleep… and before I become excommunicated by the church due to my sarcasm), it is truly wondrous that we were not scarred by some of the comments that would roll out of our mas' gubs or that we were not completely confused by what they expected from us.

Martin posted, "Are you reading that paper you're sitting on?" while Teresa offered that her ma used to say, "Hey you wee gurl. See if you fall out of that tree and break yer legs? Don't you come running to me!"

Karen reflected about one of her experiences as exchanged between a mother and child:

"Mummy, my legs are bleedin'."

"Well has it dropped off?"

"No."

"Well come back and see me when it does just that."

If we cut ourselves and resisted going through the painful process of getting the wound cleaned with an antiseptic such as Dettol and hot water or flushed with a burning sting under cold water, we were told the wound would turn into a pig's foot by the morning. As we did not want to wake up with such a thing, it was much easier to give in and go through the immediate pain, even if we were literally half bleedin' to death.

It doesn't stop there, as Turlough mentioned when she and her siblings gathered around the supper table and everyone was talking back and forth, her ma would say, "Shut yer gubs and eat your food." A feat not easily accomplished unless you know the art of osmosis. She also went on to say that when she and her siblings were out the back playing, her ma used to go to the back door and shout, "Come on in your tea is out."

When they got up from the seat they were sitting on, even if for just a moment, and we decided to sit in their place, our mothers would ask, "Would you steal my grave as quick?"

Is it any wonder that half the time we never knew whether we were coming or going? I guess that as children we also learned at a very early age that the definition of our ma's logic was "Because I said so, that's why!"

Róisín was told by her ma, "When the ice cream van comes around with the music playing it means he's no ice cream left." This reminded me of other sayings when asking for a few shillings to buy an ice cream. We were asked or bluntly told by our mums, "Do you think money grows on trees?" or, "What d'ya think I am, made of money?" Sometimes, we would be informed, "Sorry, the money man's dead."

Michelle, who shared a lot of her memories, went on to say she was often told, "If you keep leavin' things lying about your arse, how the hell d'ya expect to find them?" Tracy wrote that her ma used to say, "Get off ya, get on ya and get into yer bed." There was no questioning this whatsoever otherwise you would end up getting threatened with having the arse scalped off you or you'd get a toe up your hole for being cheeky.

Vonnie shared what she was told as a child. "Call your arse ma then you will have one of your own." Aine wrote, "My ma used to say I shoulda ate youse while yer bones were still soft." Then my sister Karen came back with, "Another one ma would say is 'He'd eat Christ off the cross and come back for the twelve apostles'," which basically meant someone who was very hungry couldn't get their food in them fast enough. This sentiment was echoed by Michelle when she posted, "That one would ate the lamb of God and come back for more!"

It seemed that Irish mothers have the gift of telepathy. My sister wrote, "Mum would say to us 'Do you think I came up the Lagan in a bubble?'" She always seemed to know where we were or what the truth was to whatever story we were trying to spin.

When asked the question, "Ma, where's so and so?" the response came back as "Up Joe's hole in America." As we heard this on a regular basis, I used to wonder how she knew that, but poor Joe must have been bunged to the doors from having so many people crammed into his cavity of closed quarters. Irish logic. You didn't dare question it!

Tracy reminded me how our mothers used to protect themselves from bill collectors by saying, "If someone's lukin' money from you, you respond with 'You can't get a pair of knickers of a bare arse.'" Now I'm not sure how our ma's thought this would work, since as children we were sent to answer the door with them shouting behind us, "Tell whoever it is I'm not home," yet their voices would be travelling through the open windies and halfway down the street for the neighbours to hear, let alone the bloke standing on the front porch.

I'm surprised those of us who grew up and heard these comments daily have any self-esteem left or that we didn't pack up our suitcases and run away with the milkman as our mas used to threaten after being constantly tortured by us, their loving children. Yet when I reflect now in my adult years, I can definitely say without any question that these were some of the best and happiest days of my life.

Our mothers weren't afraid to share their thoughts or speak their minds about the people around them or those who came into their lives, whether good or bad. As Geraldine shared, her ma would say, "Would you look at the bake on that?" This was *not* a term of endearment either.

Pauline's mum would say, "Thon face is like a busted boot, a badger's arse, or a busted sofa." Catherine, whom I quoted a little earlier, also wrote that her mum used to say, "I'd rather keep a picture of him than keep him, as he'd eat you out of house and home."

Francie let me know that one of her ma's sayings was, "They would steal the eye out of your head and come back for your eyebrows." Noleen wrote a couple on behalf of her mum: "He'd steal the milk from your tea," along with, "He's a stranger to the soap." Finally, Turlough followed up from one of her earlier posts and wrote that if someone were a miser, her ma would say, "See him? He's that stingy that if he were a ghost he wouldn't give ya a fright." And finally, my dear friend Marianne added one other thought about what her ma would come off with. "Ack, she's all fur coat and no knickers," which means what you see on the outside is definitely not indicative of a person's wealth, as this was done for show.

Many of the saying's that came to us through the mouths of our mothers must have been passed down through the generations. Tony wrote that his granny used to say, "You're getting awful big, wee fella." Martin shared, "You will regret it till yer dying day if ever ya live that long." Christine noted, "My granny always says, 'If you swallow chewing gum it will stick to yer puddins.'" Samantha shared, "If I hurt myself my nanny would say 'Far from your arse; ya don't have to sit on it. You'll be alright.'"

Charlene was often told, "Away you and chase your granny around the waterworks," which she now tells her own daughter to do the same thing.

After being scolded by my mum, my own granny used to reach for our hands and while tucking us within her arms, would say:

"Ack, don't be sayin' that to that poor wee chyle now, will ye not, Kathleen? Ack, c'mere love. C'mon you over here and see me. Don't be lisnin' to her. Sayin' that to the poor wee chyle. Ack, God love 'er. Here love, c'mon darling over here away from her. Mon, I'll make it all better for ya."

My granny became our saviour as she could save us from our ma although on the other hand, Lord Vader was a completely different story.

The final word goes to Katrina, Barbara, and the Belfast Child Facebook page. Sadly, I have been hearing that a lot of these wee sayings have been disappearing over the years, so here is a chance to breathe life back into them once more and revitalize some of the great craic and wit we would have heard as children with love from our Irish mothers:

He'd put a glass eye to sleep.
Catch yerself on, ya big lig.
Is it a dig in the gub yer after?
Go on ya wee cat ya.
Away 'n' give my head peace will ya?
Mere I'll tell you sumthin.
Bob's your uncle and Fanny's your aunt.
Go out and play you and stop your clockin'.
C'mon we'll go for a wee dander.

Stop yer yappin' or you'll get a repeat performance.

Away on outta my road or its yer head in yer hands you'll get.

Whatdya think I am, your skivvy?

Beds are for sleeping in, not jumping on.

He thinks he's funny 'cause he's a clown's face.

If you can't finish your dinner, you've no room for dessert.

If someone told you to stick your hand in a fire would ye?

Up there's for thinkin', down there's for dancin'.

Away you on and quit actin' the eejit.

Your ma's up the stairs with her head!

Take yerself off by the hand.

Spit the dummy out.

Quit yer gurnin' or I'll give you something to gurn for.

Wind your neck in.

If you don't like it, lump it.

There's no such word as can't.

I was sitting in the middle of my dinner when the door went.

Your granda is up the stairs with his stomach.

He could be in the hospital with his leg.

Get your feet on you before you go out.

How's yer arse for lovebites?

And last but not least as shared by more recently by Barbara: "This is a wee bit morbid but at wakes I heard them often say over the body, "Ach sure, he's like himself.""

This reflection is dedicated to all of the beautiful and amazing mothers and grannies back home in Belfast, throughout Ireland, and the world over. Wherever you may be, wherever you may roam, wherever you lay your heads, and as captured in the beginning words of a famous Irish poem, "May the road rise to meet you."

To those who took the time to share their own wee reflections online, I offer you this:

*Yer ma's yer da!*

## One Final Thought

IT IS OBVIOUS that I have captured some of the most difficult, yet most incredible, times of my life, including those whom I have been blessed to meet and hear their own stories of celebration, pain, jubilation, or heartbreak. Since leaving Northern Ireland twenty-eight years ago, I have been granted countless opportunities, including writing this book along with a series of funny children's books that are ready to go to a publisher for illustration. These are based on my happy childhood experiences within the Knockview and Woodford areas, learning from my mistakes while trying to do the right thing. But one thing I reflect on right now is that life is a journey that takes many twists and turns, and we never know what waits around the corner. Sometimes the reward of taking a leap of faith is greater than the risk.

In January 2012, I went through a tremendous struggle in my life and one, that by various expert medical opinions, almost claimed it. This was due to an extremely toxic work environment as bestowed upon me by individuals who seemed hell-bent on not only destroying me, but many of my colleagues in our dedication to fulfill our daily responsibilities and assigned duties. Condescending, demoralizing, and degrading are choice words that would not even come close to describing the destructive workplace environment that was created for us and in which we were expected to thrive. It was simply not humanly possible.

This brought to light an issue that is often not addressed in society, and one that is ignored even after a disclosure has been made: workplace bullying. Although efforts are being enforced to address cyber bullying due to the recent suicides of children who are faced with this destructive behaviour at the hands of others, workplace bullying holds just as much of a negative impact, and can cause a major reduction in productivity among employees who strive to maintain very high personal standards.

During this time, in the early hours of June 25, while contemplating my direction and purpose in life, I looked up flights online to go home. I had been off on medical leave for five months as a result of the work conditions that were slowly killing me. I felt totally helpless. My kids watched me suffer tremendously, but I could not function as a loving and caring father. I had to make a decision as to where I wanted to be. Either living for my children and watching and supporting them as they grew, or having them come visit me, pausing to reflect at the cemetery.

Immediately after pressing the send button to confirm my flight, I submitted my resignation. I knew I was taking a huge risk. I was walking away from a well-paying job that offered great benefits and security, but I had no quality of life left. There was no way I could go back.

Part of my healing was that I first needed to go home to recharge, as I often do. Back to a place that had brought me so much hatred and sadness, yet so much love and happiness. A place where I felt both safe yet scarred from the memories embedded within my heart, mind, and soul, due to the dark histories as locked within the North of Ireland. Regardless of these thoughts and factors, I needed to go back to both lose and find myself if I were to move forward in this journey called life.

On July 11, 2012, I touched down at Dublin airport, completely exhausted. I had not slept on the flight over due to the excitement and nervousness of going home. I stood in the parking lot and looked north and then out towards the west. I pondered my destination. Which way should I go?

Precious minutes ticked away while questions flooded my mind, and it seemed to take ages to determine the right answer. Should I go to Belfast, where I was born and raised and had loving relatives who would be overjoyed at my unannounced arrival on their doorsteps? To my land, where fires of hatred would burn throughout this very night as they have done for years, fires I witnessed and sadly participated in, almost desecrating my cultural identity? Or should I go to where I recharged myself in 1998, after my Aunt Josephine and Uncle Thomas took me to the tranquility, peace, and serenity that the West of Ireland had to offer? My heart was somewhat torn as the homesickness I'd struggled with and thought was behind me was beginning to rear its ugly head.

I ended up on the west coast, whereby one of my first determined courses of action to recharge was to go back to the Deserted Village of Slievemore at Achill Island. A place my heart and soul had yearned for years was finally within my grasp. Yet what I did not realize is that I was also about to embark **A trip through Tullymore Forest Park located near Newcastle, Northern Ireland, is a must-see for every visitor and resident. Be sure to take a trip across the stepping-stones!**

upon a journey that had occurred many years prior. A visit back to the happiness I had experienced as a child. Life was going to come full circle again. Unbeknownst to me at the time though, many little signs were also awaiting the gaze of my watchful eyes.

During his final days with us, in August 2011, I sat with my uncle Malcolm and brought his memory back to the time in 1980 when along with my aunt Maureen and cousin Treasaigh, they decided to move back to Belfast from Canada as a result of being homesick.

Since this was during the time leading up to my tenth birthday, my uncle decided that he would take Joe and me to experience our first camping and fishing trip in and around Ireland.

Prior to this, my mum had bought us a pair of fishing rods, which we would teach ourselves how to use in our front garden before venturing out to the Boghill dam with our uncle to try our luck.

And so, as I sat at his bedside, I started to share my memories about that very trip with him and some of the places he had taken us to explore.

One of the first stops he made was at breathtaking Tullymore Forest Park, as located in County Down, Northern Ireland, where we'd walk for hours and lose ourselves on the various hiking trails found here.

My uncle brought us to several historical sites and places of interest, whose meaning was unfortunately lost on us. One particular memory from that trip involved a huge mountain that appeared to have a very flat face and top. I could not shake that image from my mind. I remembered driving along roads, looking at this magnificent landscape but I had no idea where it was located.

**Standing below Ben Bulben's head in County Sligo, Ireland. This memory haunted my mind for thirty-two years.**

After that, we moved on to beautiful Buncrana, located in County Donegal, on the west coast of Ireland. It was here that Joe and I had walked along a beach for what seemed ages before finding a dead salmon lying washed up on the shore.

While checking this out, a cow on the cliff above our heads was looking over the edge, and was watching us examine the partially rotted salmon. It began mooing down to us. For whatever reason inspired us to do so, we decided to moo back at it before saying, "Ack, go on you auld cow ye."

Being the cheeky wee frigger that he was, Joe took some stones from the beachfront and threw them up at the cow. Thankfully the stones never got near it due to the height of the cliff.

In 1980, I can be seen here with my brother Joe taking a trip across those very stepping-stones. Joe forever left his footprint on the tranquility of Tullymore Forest Park.

Lo and behold, the cow took immediate exception to his actions. It pulled its head back and what seemed to be almost on command, the cow backed its arse up to the edge of the cliff. Without warning, it lifted its tail and empted the contents of its bowels.

The two of us scattered like ants, running full speed in opposite directions so as to not get covered by the incoming shite targeted at our heads. That was the last time that Joe would ever challenge a cow to a duel.

In Buncrana, Joe and I explored a campground we would be staying at and went into a building that had a TV. Excited as we were, about to sit down to watch our favourite programs and after turning the set on, we were horrified that it was not in the

English language that we had been taught our entire lives, but a language completely foreign to my ears at the time. Gaelic.

I looked at Joe for answers, as I could not comprehend how there was a completely different language in our country. I did not understand that there was a difference between Northern and Southern Ireland, even though the money we had brought with us was referred to as Irish. I also didn't give much appreciation to what was on the TV, and turned it off as it made no sense to me whatsoever.

And so, after my uncle passed on September 11, 2011, I stood over his coffin at his memorial viewing and made a vow to him that the next time I went home I would honour his memory and go back to some of those places he took us as kids. It was as if the landscape was calling for my return. I asked for his guidance and for him to watch over me, as I only had the memories from that trip.

★★★★★

Back to July 15, 2012. After packing up my supplies for the journey ahead of me and while still trying to find myself after leaving behind the toxic work environment, I departed early that morning to embark upon an adventure that would require the entire day and then some.

I headed east, but as I drove along the N5 motorway, I found myself stuck in very heavy traffic congestion. Since I did not want to waste precious time, I studied my road map of Ireland and tried to find the first shortcut I could detour onto, away from the backlog of vehicles ahead of me.

While following this unplanned route and making my way into the first town I came across, I happened to be stopped at a T-junction. Before I could release the clutch and without warning, a police motorbike seemingly came zooming out of nowhere and blocked my path. "Great. What's going on here?" I wondered.

Suddenly, hundreds upon hundreds of cyclists went zooming past me on a training tour of Western Ireland. I gasped at the sight of this and immediately reflected upon its meaning.

The night before, after visiting Achill, I met a man named Gerry in the town of Castlebar who had cycled up to a McDonalds drive-thru window to place an order. He was from County Derry, and as we spoke, I told him I was born and raised in Belfast and was home from Canada on a trip to heal my spirit. He mentioned that he was on a cycling tour and was part of the Phoenix Cycling Club.

At this point my mouth went bone dry. My mum's brother Jimmy was also a part of this club. My mum regularly told me that I was his double both in looks and in his ways of interacting with his family, whom he loved by all accounts. He always asked, "Where's your pins?" and would give us dead legs, leaving us partially paralyzed in the process for ten minutes or so.

James "Jimmy" Devlin, my mum's brother and my uncle, who was tragically taken from us in 1987 while undertaking one of his greatest passions in life: riding his bike. I was always told that I take after him both in looks and his playful mannerisms.

My mum always said that my uncle's memory would never be at rest so long as I was alive. She never did get over his death. In my mind, here was my uncle and my mum guiding me while I was trying to find myself again. They were letting me know, just as my uncle Jimmy had done when he came back for my mum along with the rest of her family and stood at the end of my bed when her time came for a new journey, that they too were watching over and guiding me while I was seeking to recharge my spirit. I carefully followed the cyclists for ten miles and reflected on happy memories with the knowledge that they were here with me.

Much further into my trip I was coming into County Sligo. I would need to make my way to County Donegal, where we had done much of our camping as kids. I pulled over a few miles up the road in the sleepy community of Rath Chormaic to stretch my legs from driving, only to find myself lost and inspired by the beautiful scenery around me. I took a few pictures.

Continuing along the road into the town of Drumcliff, and while lost in my own thoughts and reflections, I happened to catch a fleeting glimpse of a sign on the side of the road that made me stop the car in an instant, pause for a few moments, and while looking in the rear view mirror, try to catch my breath as if I had just run an marathon. Could it be?

I turned the car around, all the while my heart raced and beat like a bass drum with tremendous adrenaline flushes. Had it have not been for my chest and its skeletal cage structure, I'm sure my heart would have jumped out of its cavity and rushed over to read the sign itself.

Exactly thirty-two years to the day prior and on my tenth birthday, my uncle Malcolm had brought my brother Joe and me to visit not just a historic landmark, but this was the grave of one of Ireland's most famous poets. This was the final resting place of William Butler Yeats.

When there as kids at ages ten and eleven, we did not take into account the significance of where we were or what any of it meant. We stood around his grave and got our photos taken like any other child would do when told to stand still and pose for a picture.

**My brother at the grave of one of Ireland's most famous poets – William Butler Yeats.**

However, this day also happened to be my forty-second birthday. Here I was about to pay homage to a famous and brilliant Irish poet, while remembering and paying respects to honour the life of my uncle and his outstanding ability to recite poetry to us. I was awestruck, as it seemed that life was not just throwing coincidental patterns at me, but was also giving me its own guidance that I was here to lose myself, find myself, and try to understand that within the mysteries of life, there is so much meaning to be had, no matter the struggles we face each day and the difficult choices we must make to better ourselves.

In the written words of W.B. Yeats:

*Under bare Ben Bulben's head*
*In Drumcliff churchyard Yeats is laid.*
*An ancestor was rector there*
*Long years ago, a church stands near,*
*By the road an ancient cross.*
*No marble, no conventional phrase;*
*On limestone quarried near the spot*
*By his command these words are cut:*
*Cast a cold eye*
*On life, on death.*
*Horseman, pass by!*

While visiting the gravesite, I looked around for someone to take a picture of me. There was a lady sitting beside the church reading a book but I chose to not interrupt her. Within about five minutes, there was a group of tourists that came walking up. I did not want to disengage them from their own interests and sightseeing activities.

Reflecting and lost in thought again, a tour guide from Germany happened to come by, and we spoke about the significance of this day and the meaning behind my spiritual journey home to recharge and re-energize myself. This was related to a book I had read by James Redfield called *The Celestine Prophecy,* which he had also read. As Redfield explains, there are no coincidences in life but reasons why everything happens. Just as the reason that on this very day I had gotten stuck in traffic and had to take a detour; just as the reason for having hundreds of cyclists stop me in my tracks; and finally, the reason for me stopping outside the town of Rath Chormaic to take a few pictures and stretch my legs. Had this series of events not occurred as they did, neither would the chance meeting to say hello to someone from a culture very much removed from my own. A person who understood and appreciated the sense of a spiritual being through his own eyes, and the journey life takes us on.

But what also had haunted my mind for years was the massive mountain in what seemed to be the middle of nowhere. I shared with the gentleman how I remembered it as a child from that fateful day of July 15, 1980, and how it looked very impressive in its might and beauty.

The tour guide looked at me and said, "You're talking about Ben Bulben's head as Yeats has written about in his piece here. You're almost there. It's just down the road from us." He pointed out the direction I would need to go to find it. Finally, dreams and memories that had haunted my mind all of these years were within sight.

I smiled, fully aware that regardless of the baggage that had been dragging me down, these issues were now going to be put behind me. Once again, I needed to move forward with renewed strength and determination. The signs that had been bestowed upon me up to this point were not finished just yet.

Upon reaching County Donegal, driving through the various villages and towns with shop fronts bustling with locals and tourists alike and getting much deeper into the back areas of this breathtaking part of home, I made my way from Ardara up towards the seaside town of Portnoo. It was on a lonely stretch of road that I knew I was going to be okay.

I found myself driving along narrow roads that were barely designed to take one vehicle, let alone two. As I navigated the road, I found it strange that as this was literally in middle of nowhere, another car was coming toward me. Luckily, a tiny cut-out had been made either side of the road to allow for two vehicles to slip ever so closely and trickily past one another, which was no easy feat to do. As we did this, the driver of the other car looked at me as I did him.

It was as if time stood still for an eternity: the driver of that vehicle was a spitting image of my uncle Malcolm. An older gentleman with white hair and matching beard, soft blue eyes, and a checkered shirt like my uncle wore. He stared deeply into my soul as I returned the acknowledgement. As our cars inched forward and cleared one another, I had barely released the clutch only to hear myself say aloud, "Did you see that?" I thought that perhaps I was trying to fill the void, locking eyes with the first person who looked like him, but then I realized that people regularly mistake me for someone *they* know.

I never did find the place where my uncle had taken Joe and me fishing. With all the other chance findings of buried treasures and sights of discovery in Ardara, and the seaside village of Portnoo, I never made it to Buncrana either.

I finally got back from this adventure around half-three in the morning as I ended up missing my turn and wound up in the middle of nowhere in County Galway, only to be rescued by two ladies who helped me find my way back to the motorway. Thankfully, I also found a twenty-four hour petrol station, as I was on fumes.

July 20, 2012 with Barry Devlin of legendary Irish band, Horslips.

The following morning I continued my journey throughout my homeland, stopping unannounced at the homes of family and friends, iPad in hand and waiting to record the gobsmacked looks on their faces. My cousin Adele shattered the sound barrier and woke up the whole of sleepy Newcastle, County Down, Northern Ireland with her screams and expletives seeing me standing at the bottom of her footpath. I am sure the locals must have thought that a Banshee was out on the prowl.

During this same trip, Pat McManus, his beautiful wife Sallie, Barry Devlin of Horslips, and 150 of Pat's closest friends would join him to celebrate thirty years in the history marking one of his most famous songs ever written, "Needle in the Groove." Although having recorded two concert dvds prior, Pat was pursuing his lifetime dream of recording a live concert from Ireland as captured in Drogheda, County Louth.

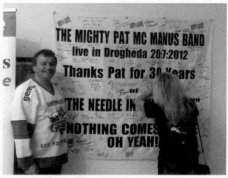

The banner developed to recognize Pat's dedication to the music industry and to celebrate recording his first *Live from Ireland* DVD, which is available for purchase on the Pat McManus band website: http://www.patmcmanus.co.uk/

In order for that to happen, I had picked up a ticket to attend this show on the same night I bought my plane ticket and had submitted my resignation. I kept my attendance a secret and shocked the life out of Molly by pulling one of John's stunts, as I had told them in advance that I would not be able to come to the show.

One last chance to say cheerio to Pat McManus after the Drogheda show had wrapped up filming for the night.

After leaving their family homestead in Derrylin, County Fermanagh, I was waiting to turn out onto the road towards Belfast when a vehicle drove by.

I nearly jumped out of my skin. By sheer coincidence or perhaps yet another sign, the driver of that vehicle and his passenger were Pat and Sallie McManus, who were en route to Drogheda to set up and prepare for the concert two days later. When they stopped briefly at a petrol station further along the road, I pulled up behind them, parked my car, and walked over to the driver door before giving it a wee knock.

Pat almost came through the window, welcoming me with open arms, hugging the dear life out of me, and asking what I was doing there, as word had also filtered to him that I was not coming over and would not be attending the show. A few moments later, Sallie got back into the vehicle and was just as shocked as Pat was but delighted to see me. Talk about a welcome home!

I joined the Pat McManus band on Friday, July 20, for sound check. The concert thereafter was brilliant by all accounts. The show included a dedication Pat wrote in memory of the late Gary Moore called "Belfast Boy," and was opened on stage by a uilleann pipe player. Marty McDermott on bass and Paul "Faloonatic" Faloon on drums round out the musicians who make up the band and have become dear friends. Keith Muir, the keyboardist from the band the Quireboys, joined the band onstage for this special night.

A few days later, I would return to Canada, feeling completely renewed. I was ready to take on the next chapter of my life in whatever form that would be. I left all of the negative influences that made me decide to go home in the first place, behind me once and for all.

In trying to fit all of this together, from first writing this book to these final few sentences, I have realized that life is a never-ending journey of exploration, and of learning, and provides us with signs along our path that help guide us. These signs let us know that we are never given more than what we can handle. Life is made up of wonderful and difficult moments. The search for self-identity cannot be forcefully completed within a defined timeframe.

It made me realize that this life I've been given is one that needs to be lived to the fullest if I am hopeful to make change in this world for my two children, Caitlin and Ciarán, and for others who come into my life through either personal or professional engagements.

It made me realize that my existence as a son, a brother, a father, a friend, a social worker, but most importantly, as a fellow human being, along with my interactions with other people, whether friends, family, or complete strangers, are not merely coincidences. Each of them brings a special meaning and are a part of my onward journey.

And finally it made me realize—as Elder Raven helped me rediscover in 2005 after the death of my beloved mum—that in my darkest moments, all I had to do was reach out and ask for help, as someone was there to listen to my story. Just as you have done.

**My wonderful children, Ciarán and Caitlin, who were with me here on a family holiday back to the place where I first landed in 1985: Toronto, Canada.**

★★★★★

I once heard that I am not a human having a spiritual experience but that I am a spirit having a human experience. With that said, this is my life, in which I can help tell the stories of others who continue to define my worldviews through poems. This is my life, which I have looked back upon through my own personal reflections. This is my life, as seen through the eyes of a Belfast child.

Godspeed, Madiba

O N DECEMBER 5, 2013, a deafening roar of silence fell upon the ears of the world. Millions of people wept what some might consider to be enough tears that could create an ocean filled with human grief, while others celebrated in song, dance, and prayer, to honour the legacy of a gentle and noble man: Nelson Rolihlahla Mandela.

Nelson Mandela, a man who became the first black President of South Africa, was lovingly known to his people as Madiba, the name for the clan of which he was a member. Madiba died at his home while he was surrounded by the love, warmth, and support of his family. Although the world knew for many months that his health was failing him as a result of recurring lung infections due to contracting Tuberculosis while he was imprisoned, it did not lessen the impact of his death when announced.

Mr. Mandela was also known by another name, "Tata," which means "father" and is a term of endearment that South Africans and others around the world bestowed upon him regardless of their age, as they seen him as a father figure. He was a man who fought with inconceivable perseverance and determination to end apartheid—the legalized racially motivated segregation of people imposed by the ruling white minority South African government within his beloved country, until 1994.

In facing the death penalty at the conclusion of the Rivonia trial and prior to being sentenced to life imprisonment on April

20, 1964, and just like the words to the end of his now famous "Speech from the Dock" that lasted more than four hours to the court, the voice of Nelson Mandela became immortalized in human history. His words instill the same profound impact to this day upon generations of people as they did on the day they were first spoken from his lips:

> "During my lifetime I have dedicated myself to this struggle of the African people. I have fought against white domination, and I have fought against black domination. I have cherished the ideal of a democratic and free society in which all persons live together in harmony and with equal opportunities. It is an ideal for which I hope to live and to see realised. But, My Lord, if it needs be, it is an ideal for which I am prepared to die."

The fierce, personal conviction that Nelson Mandela held was one without hatred, resentment, or anger, and is a true testament of the man who would not allow his spirit to become fragmented or broken by his imprisonment in his quest for a democratic and free society, and one without oppression or racial domination.

Madiba sought reconciliation and urged forgiveness for the government that imprisoned him, and inspired nations the world over after he negotiated an end to segregation through his anti-apartheid movement. His prison sentence, which lasted twenty-seven years until his release on February 11, 1990, was also captured in another one of his famous quotes:

> "As I walked out the door to the gate that would lead to my freedom, I knew if I didn't leave my bitterness and hatred behind, I'd still be in prison."

Since we will all grieve on the passing of Nelson Mandela in our own way, I pause for a moment to reflect on what his teachings meant to me. Each and every one of us who knew, were influenced by, or touched in such a way through the words of wisdom that Madiba expressed beyond his ninety-five years on this earth, a man who has left such an everlasting legacy in trying to define what the true meaning of humanity is all about, even in the face of adversity, that we, as one race of people, must continue to embody the gifts that he has left for us all if we are to strive in our efforts to define ourselves as being truly human.

The everlasting gift that I feel through Madiba's own aspirations is for me to try to measure up to the knowledge and courage that he freely shared in how to be a better person, and to promote those teachings to help create a world in which we are all seen as being equal to each other.

If we, as a people, who have been defined by socially constructed hatred against others who are different from us by way of appearance, culture, race, religious beliefs, political affiliations, social standing, or sexual orientation, others who breathe the same air that we inhale, who shed the same tears that we cry, and who bleed the same colour of blood as us, then we, as a people, must begin to look at ourselves as to what we aspire to do in order to help benefit those who are less fortunate than ourselves before our time comes to die. We can be the difference in making global change.

Should we fail to do that and if we continue to be greedy, then we will never know the gift of giving. If we continue to embrace hate, then we will never know the magic of love. And if we continue to wage war against our fellow humans, we will never know the sanctity of peace.

Is this the legacy that we ourselves wish to leave behind for others to know and remember us by? Or, do we hope to fulfill a life to help and teach others in the way that Madiba has taught us? For me, one of those teachings is to ensure that those who are less fortunate have their basic human rights and dignity recognized, and without oppressing someone else to realize our own successes in life.

Once again, and in the famous words of Nelson Mandela on racism as spoken in his autobiography, *Long Walk to Freedom*, published in 1994:

> "No one is born hating another person because of the colour of his skin, or his background, or his religion. People must learn to hate, and if they can learn hate, then they can be taught to love, for love comes more naturally to the human heart than its opposite."

As we continue to mourn and celebrate your life under a veil of death, but in your own words as taken from an interview for the 1996 Academy award-nominated documentary that bears your namesake, I believe that this is a most fitting tribute which captures the spirit of who you were, and what you meant to each and every one of us who pause to reflect:

> "Death is something inevitable. When a man has done what he considers to be his duty to his people and his country, he can rest in peace. I believe I have made that effort and that is, therefore, why I will sleep for the eternity."

It is truly a great honour for me to dedicate this personal reflection to the legacy of Mr. Nelson Rolihlahla Mandela, who has been released from this life and awaits us all in the next. My hope is that we continue to embrace his courage, strength, humility, passion, wisdom, nobility, and profound teachings to forgive our oppressors, in that we may inspire and empower this generation and those who lie behind us, to ensure that the world in which we all exist together as human beings can prosper as equals to one another, without prejudice or persecution.

Godspeed, Madiba.
1918 – 2013.

# Special Note to the Reader

I've learned that even with the most dedicated of efforts, one person simply cannot accomplish making a difference in this world alone. As the old saying goes, "many hands to make light work." Therefore, by purchasing this book, you are helping me make a dream come true in that I will be donating a portion of the royalties received to selected charities that are near and dear to my heart.

Every donation, no matter how big or small, comes from the heart and goes a long way. If you are able, please consider making a donation to a charity of your choice. Every penny counts in striving for global change!

Mo chara, go raibh maith agat / My friend, thank you very much.

Greg.

GREG MCVICKER RECEIVED his Bachelor of Social Work degree from the University of Manitoba in 2008. He has consulted, wrote scripts, developed, as well as produced and co-produced both Pandemic and HIV awareness videos for the sixty-three First Nation communities in Manitoba. He then followed this up by scripting, developing, and producing his own series of animated videos to create and promote additional awareness on HIV featuring the world's greatest advocates as his primary characters in the fight against this disease. They are available online: friggermortis YouTube.

Greg resides in Winnipeg, Canada with his two children, Caitlin and Ciarán. Through the Eyes of a

Belfast Child is his first book. He has written a series of children's books called, The Adventures of Silly Billy. These are based on his real life experiences while growing up in Belfast, and learning from his mistakes. He hopes to work with an illustrator and have these published soon.

Greg aspires to expand his efforts to address HIV on a global level by ensuring equitable access to antiretroviral medications for those nations where this preventable disease is most prevalent. He likens this personal mission to the inspirational efforts U2's Bono has done through (RED).

# Connect with the Author

AS I MENTIONED to you in my opening notes to you, the reader, I would love to hear your story, for who knows what kind of higher learning or healing can come from it, or how it can help support someone else by knowing that they are not alone in their journey of life.

If you are interested in connecting with me, please feel free to do so. I make every effort to respond to all enquiries within a timely manner, and certainly look forwards to hearing from you!

| | |
|---|---|
| **Facebook:** | facebook.com/ThroughtheEyesofaBelfastChild |
| **Email:** | BelfastChild@shaw.ca |
| **Twitter:** | @BelfastChild70 |
| **Hashtag:** | #BelfastChild |